READING
TECHNIQUES
FOR FCE

CLARE WEST

WITH
KEY

GEORGIAN PRESS

Georgian Press (Jersey) Limited
8 Duhamel Place
St Helier
Jersey JE1 3WF
Channel Islands

© Clare West 1997

First published by Georgian Press (Jersey) Limited 1997

ISBN 1-873630-14-X (without key)
ISBN 1-873630-15-8 (with key)

Produced by AMR Limited

Printed in Great Britain

Contents

Acknowledgements

The author and publishers are grateful for permission to reproduce copyright material on the following pages:

Pages 57 and 58: 'TV exposure damages children's speech', and the extract from 'Volunteers for a leisure America', from *Guardian Weekly*, by permission of *The Guardian*.

Page 60: Extract from *My Early Life* by Winston Churchill (Hamlyn 1930), by permission of HarperCollins Publishers Limited.

Page 70: Extracts from the Empire State Building information brochure, by permission of Helmsley-Spear, Inc.

Page 74: Extract from *The Seven Wonders of the Ancient World* by Hugh Gethin & Judith Brown (Georgian Press (Jersey) Limited 1994). © Hugh Gethin and Judith Brown, 1994.

Page 76: Adapted article 'My kind of day' by Judi Dench from *Radio Times*, by permission of BBC Worldwide Limited.

Page 78: Extract from *George Fisher Update*, by permission of George Fisher Limited.

Page 84: Extract from 'Waiting game is strictly for pros', from *Guardian Weekly*, by permission of *The Guardian*.

Page 86: Extract from *Adventures in Two Worlds* by A.J. Cronin (Gollancz 1952), by permission of A.M. Heath & Co. Limited. © A.J. Cronin.

Pages 88 & 94: Extracts from 'Amazing life of the old man of the sea' and 'Is life really just a game of chance?' from *The Daily Mail*, by permission of Solo Syndication. © Daily Mail/Solo Syndication.

Page 96: Adapted article 'My kind of day' by Sue Lloyd-Roberts from *Radio Times*, by permission of BBC Worldwide Limited.

Page 98: Extract from 'Work till you drop' from *The Guardian*, by permission.

Page 101: Extracts from 'London in winter' by Robin Mead, reproduced from *20:20*, the West Coast InterCity magazine, 12.95, by permission of the author. © Robin Mead, 1995.

Page 104: Extract from 'Thieves cut off in their crime' from *The Daily Mail*, by permission of Solo Syndication. © Daily Mail/Solo Syndication.

Page 106: Extract from *As I Walked Out One Midsummer Morning* by Laurie Lee, by permission of Penguin Books Limited. © Laurie Lee, 1969.

Although every effort has been made to contact copyright holders, this has not been possible in the cases listed below. We will be pleased to rectify any errors or omissions at the earliest opportunity.

Page 46: 'The Village That Vanished' from *World of Strange Phenomena Omnibus* by Charles Berlitz (Warner Books 1995).

Pages 62 and 108: The adapted articles 'The National Trust' (10.95) and 'Venice' (2.95) from *National Geographic*.

Page 111: The extracts from *New Zealand – a Lonely Planet travel survival kit* (Lonely Planet Publications 1995).

Photographs

Pages 62, 71, 101, 108: Greg Evans International.
Pages 75, 112: Zefa Pictures Limited.
Pages 85: Magnum Photos Limited.

Cover design by George Mansolas.

Who is this book for?

Reading Techniques for FCE is for students at upper-intermediate level who wish to improve their general reading skills in English and/or work specifically towards Paper 1 of the revised Cambridge First Certificate examination (FCE). It can be used to supplement any coursebook at this level, and is suitable for use in the classroom, for homework, or (in the case of the With Key edition) for self-study.

What does *Reading Techniques for FCE* offer?

The book aims to provide:

* coverage of the five major reading skills required at this level – skimming for gist, scanning for information, intensive reading, reading between the lines and speed reading

* extensive practice of all relevant task-types – multiple matching, completing gapped texts, summarizing and multiple choice

* texts and tasks carefully graded throughout

* clear guidelines in study boxes

* regular reminders of techniques already covered

* two sections of predominantly authentic texts, including four exam practice tests

* a user-friendly, attractive layout, so that the material is accessible and a pleasure to use.

How is the book organised?

It is divided into four distinct sections:

Section 1   SKILLS ANALYSIS (8 units)

In this section eight reading skills or task-types are presented, with examples and practice exercises in the relevant techniques. In addition there are four short Progress Tests, each with feedback for extra help with corrections.

Section 2   READING TECHNIQUES IN USE (4 units)

The units in this section cover the four parts of the FCE Reading Paper, explaining clearly which techniques are required for each type of task. Practice exercises all look similar to real exam ones, but they are shorter and easier. Each unit is followed by a Progress Test.

Section 3   APPROACHING THE EXAM (4 units)

As in Section 2, the four units deal with the four parts of the FCE Reading Paper, but here the texts are mostly authentic and the tasks as relevant as possible to FCE. Texts are slightly shorter and more accessible than in the real exam.

Section 4   EXAM PRACTICE (4 tests)

This section allows students to make use of all they have learnt so far, and to gain valuable practice for FCE Paper 1. There are four exam-format Practice Tests, with full-length texts and tasks appropriate to FCE level and specifications.

How should *Reading Techniques for FCE* be used?

As the texts have been carefully selected and graded for level, it is better to start at the beginning and work consistently through the book. It is important to check answers in the Key or with a teacher, to do the Progress Tests and complete the feedback pages, and to go back and do the exercises again at a later date if necessary. Only when Sections 1-3 have been completed and thoroughly understood should the Exam Practice section be attempted.

Tips for the teacher

Make yourself familiar with the differences between the various reading skills. Always bear the particular aim of the unit in mind when presenting it to your class, in order to focus students' attention on it.

Take the exercises slowly at first and don't be in a hurry to get through the units. Reading techniques are not learnt quickly, and students need time to get used to using them. Remember that these skills may be completely new to them.

Help your students to take some responsibility for their learning by encouraging them to use the feedback pages and student's note boxes and to refer back to earlier study boxes.

Tips for the student

- Read the study boxes carefully and try to follow the guidelines in them.

- Use a pencil to complete the exercises, so that if you need to do them again later you can simply rub out your first set of answers.

- Always ask if you don't understand *why* you made a mistake, or look back at the study box to find the reason.

- Reading is one of the most valuable ways of improving your English, so read whatever you enjoy, as often as possible – newspapers, magazines, short stories, novels and so on.

Finally ...

I hope you will find *Reading Techniques for FCE* useful and stimulating. It should make reading English easier and therefore more fun for the student, as well as providing valuable preparation for FCE. I hope it will smooth the teacher's path too.

Clare West

Cambridge FCE Paper 1 is in four parts. Each part consists of one or more texts (usually one), with comprehension exercises.

Types of texts

Texts will be authentic or as close to authentic as possible and may come from advertisements, brochures, correspondence, fiction, guidebooks, manuals, messages, magazine and newspaper articles, reports and other sources.

Task formats

The tasks involved will be:

- **multiple matching** (where students have to match headings or summaries with paragraphs in a text, or questions with their answers in a text)

- **completing gapped texts** (where students are asked to put missing sentences or paragraphs into a text with gaps)

- **multiple choice** (where students are required to choose the correct answer out of four alternatives).

Reading skills required

The following reading skills will be needed:

- **skimming** for gist or overview

- **scanning** for specific information

- **intensive reading** for detailed understanding

- **reading between the lines** or deducing meaning

- **speed reading**.

Structure and marks

The parts of the Reading Paper are as follows:

Part 1 – multiple matching questions (headings or summaries), followed by a text

Part 2 – a text followed by multiple choice comprehension questions (A, B, C or D)

Part 3 – a text with gaps, followed by the missing sentences or paragraphs plus one extra which does not fit perfectly

Part 4 – multiple matching and multiple choice questions followed by a text.

The total number of questions is 35, numbered consecutively 1-35 throughout the paper. There are two marks for each question in Parts 1, 2 and 3, and one mark for each question in Part 4, so that each part is worth approximately an equal number of marks.

Timing

The overall time allowed for Paper 1 is 1 hour 15 minutes, so each part needs to be completed in about 15 minutes, in order to allow time for checking and transferring answers to the examination answer sheet.

Skimming for gist

> If you want to know roughly what a text is about, you read it through quickly – this is
> **skimming**. You let your eye run over it, rather like throwing a flat stone on to a lake, so
> that it just skims the surface. Then you should have **the gist**, that is, the general meaning,
> without any of the details.

A Look quickly at this short text and say briefly what it is about, in your own words, in one
sentence. Do not read every word. Use the guidance to help you.

We usually went by bus, but sometimes if we wanted to save our bus fares for some project or
other, we went on foot. Of course, this took much longer, but we followed the bus route, all the
way down Dyke Road to the shops at the roundabout, and then heading down Montpelier Road
towards the sea, past the town houses with their neat window boxes, St Michael's Church with
its tall spire, and the solid, well-built Lloyds Bank building on the corner, until we reached the
school.

☞ GUIDANCE

What tense should you use?

B Do the same with this text.

It seems that most of us want more holidays than we actually get, apart from a small number of
workaholics who do not take all the days off they are entitled to. It is important, however,
according to the experts, to make sure that you use your time off sensibly, to relax and unwind
from the pressures of the daily routine. Some holidays can be more exhausting than work, so it
is crucial to plan the kind of holiday that is appropriate for your personal needs.

☞ GUIDANCE

1 What is the topic in one word?

2 What advice is being given?

3 What does 'crucial' mean?

C Do the same with this text.

The old woman looked at the pale faces under the parasols, and sniffed scornfully. In her day
they hadn't worried about the hole in the ozone layer. Well, there probably hadn't been one
then. She remembered slapping coconut oil on and lying on the beach, sizzling almost, in the
baking sun. Now it was barrier cream, Factor 25, and sunhats all the time. 'And we used to eat
whatever we fancied, too,' she thought. 'It never did us any harm.' Things weren't what they
used to be.

☞ GUIDANCE

What are the two times or periods mentioned?

D Do the same with this text.

The recent expansion of tourist development in Spain has brought about a decline in long-established agricultural methods. Young people are no longer prepared to tend the olives and the vines, when higher salaries are being offered by the construction and service industries.

☞ GUIDANCE

1 Can you think of an adjective that describes a long-established custom, beginning with **t**?

2 Which tenses are used in the text?

3 Ask yourself – What is happening? Where? Why?

E Do the same with this text.

A shortage of rainfall in parts of Europe has meant restrictions on water consumption for many residents and, consequently, greater interest in the conservation of what is, after all, one of our most valuable resources. Water companies are investing considerable amounts in the maintenance and improvement of their reservoirs and pipework, and many individual consumers now collect rainwater for their gardens in water butts and tanks.

☞ GUIDANCE

1 Don't worry about vocabulary details like 'reservoirs', 'butts'.

2 Find another word/expression for 'shortage of rainfall'.

3 Ask yourself – What has happened? Where? Why? What is the result?

F Do the same with this text.

Every year, air pollution in Paris is at its worst during holiday weekends, especially in July, when most people leave by car for their holiday destination, and at the end of August, when they return. To combat this, new transport measures are being introduced by the authorities, including the building of a new tram line for southern Paris, a ban on Sunday traffic in several streets, and an ambitious plan for 56 km of cycle tracks and new pedestrian zones. There has even been a proposal, supported by the mayor of Paris, that public transport should be free on days when pollution reaches a dangerous level; ozone readings would be taken and public announcements would be made on radio and television, to let people know. Not only are the Paris authorities trying to prevent the chaos caused by public transport strikes in the past, they also want to be able to guarantee safe air for everyone.

☞ GUIDANCE

1 What do 'combat', 'measures' and 'guarantee' mean?

2 When is this problem 'at its worst'?

3 Is this text mainly about public transport, or air pollution? Look at the beginning and end of the text.

Scanning for information

> **Scanning** is a reading technique used only when you need to find answers to specific questions. Often the answers are short and factual, and may be numbers or names. If the text is long, you may not have time to read all of it in order to find your answers. Look carefully at the questions first, decide which general topic they refer to, then let your eye run over the text until it is caught by a relevant section or paragraph. Concentrate on this section only, to find the answers.

A Read these questions, which refer to the advertisements which follow. Do not answer the questions yet.

1 Where could you send your children for a holiday?
2 Which company offers the cheapest flight to Vancouver?
3 Where can you go to the circus?
4 Where can you watch Scottish dancing?
5 Which new release is about a magician's assistant?
6 Where can you do some wine-tasting?
7 Which company offers boating holidays?
8 Where can you buy traditional roses?
9 Who would like to meet a girl who is interested in music?
10 Where can you buy antiques?

Which of these categories of advertisement (A-H) do questions 1-10 refer to? Write the appropriate letter(s) next to each question. You may use some letters more than once.

A air fares	B fairs & shows	C holidays	D music festivals
E films	F personal	G gardening	H do-it-yourself

B Now answer the 10 questions above by scanning the advertisements for the answers.

FILMS - NEW RELEASES

BLUE IN THE FACE (15)
Stories and jokes about Brooklyn life. Indulgent companion piece to *Smoke*, with Harvey Keitel, Roseanne, and many cameos. Director, Wayne Wang.
Plaza (0171-437-1234)
Renoir (0171-837-8402)
Richmond (0181-332-0030)
Ritzy (0171-737-2121)
Warner West End (0171-437-4343)

ROUGH MAGIC (12)
Magician's assistant Bridget Fonda finds true magic in Mexico. Engaging oddity from director Clare Peploe. With Russell Crowe.
Odeons:
(01426-915-353) *Haymarket*
(01426-914-666) *Kensington*
(01426-914-098)*Swiss Cottage*

HOLIDAYS

Parents Are your children bored during the summer holidays? Camp Beaumont – Day & residential camps. Brochure 0171 724 2233

BRITAIN'S BEST
BOATING
There is still time to book your Boating Holidays on all Britain's finest waterways. Including Norfolk Broads, Canals, Thames, Cambs and Scotland. Short breaks too! Quote B2329.
FREEPHONE 0800 520 520.
HOSEASONS

RED ROSE COTTAGES Super self-catering in Forest of Bowland & Lancashire. Explore pretty villages, countryside, heritage & coast. 01200 27310

FAIRS/SHOWS

LONDON
Adams Antiques Fair
Ideal opportunity to see and buy silver, jewellery, glass, porcelain, furniture and other decorative items.
Royal Horticultural Society Halls, Greycoat Street, SW1 (0171-834-4333). Tomorrow, 9.30am-4.30pm; adults £3, children 50p.

BELFAST
Ballysillan Carnival Day
Featuring stalls, demonstrations and activities for all the family.
Ballysillan Leisure Centre (01232 391040). Today, midday-6pm; admission free.

BRIGHTON
Chinese State Circus
Famous circus returns with some spellbinding action that includes 14 girls balancing on one bicycle.
The Big Top, Preston Park, Preston Street (01273 709709). Today, tomorrow, times vary: £5.

BUILTH WELLS
Annual Festival of Scottish Dance
Enjoy a spectacular weekend of demonstrations and performances.
Wyeside Arts Centre, Castle Street (01982 552555). Today, tomorrow, times vary; telephone for details.

HALIFAX
UNICEF Music Day
Charity celebration with a range of musical events.
Piece Hall, (01422-358086).
Tomorrow, midday-3pm; free.

MAIDSTONE
Festival of English Food and Wine
Family entertainment including stalls, demonstrations and puppet shows. Also wine tasting and food tasting and, on Sunday only, a presentation by the celebrity television chef Michael Barry.
Leeds Castle, (01622 880 008).
Today, tomorrow, 10am-5pm; £6, child £3.70.

AIR FARES

Canada

From Gatwick, Manchester, B'mnghm, E Mids, Glasgow

TORONTO	**£169**
MONTREAL	**£169**
HALIFAX	**£219**
WINNIPEG	**£249**
VANCOUVER	**£249**
CALGARY	**£249**
EDMONTON	**£249**

Canadian Affair ATOL 3971
589 Fulham Road London SW6

0171 385 4400

CURRENT BEST BUYS ON THE WORLD'S FINEST AIRLINES

(excl. taxes)	one way	return from		one way	return from
SYDNEY	£329	£469	NEW YORK	£115	£175
PERTH	£314	£544	BOSTON	£129	£199
AUCKLAND	£352	£615	FLORIDA	£159	£269
BANGKOK	£198	£384	LOS ANGELES	£195	£239
HONG KONG	£237	£384	SAN FRANCISCO	£195	£271
SINGAPORE	£225	£384	TORONTO	£138	£234
BALI	£264	£439	VANCOUVER	£311	£311
SAIGON	£297	£495	CARIBBEAN	£175	£334
TOKYO	£286	£545	MEXICO CITY	£253	£352
DELHI	£211	£341	KATHMANDU	£265	£473

Trailfinders

194 Kensington High Street, London W8 7RG
Long Haul Flights: 0171-938 3939
First & Business Class: 0171-938 3444

PERSONAL

ORIENTAL LADY, 30s, tall, elegant, attractive, brainy, well-educated, professional, seeks compatible gentleman. London. Box 1299.

FARMER, 40, seeks good-looking girl who enjoys country and classical music. Midlands. Box 2199.

ATTRACTIVE MALE, 36, fun loving, successful, sporty, great sense of humour, seeks Miss Right. Photo please. Box 0999.

GARDENING

Old-fashioned and English roses – 700 varieties.
Free catalogue.
David Austin, Albrighton, Wolverhampton WV7 3HB

When you start a test in this book, remember to:

- read this study box first to find out what reading skills you need
- read the instructions (the rubric) very carefully
- concentrate hard on doing the test, with no distractions!

The following test is to see how well you can **scan for information** (see Unit 2).

Remember   – look carefully at the questions first
    – decide which general topic they refer to
    – **scan** the text for the right topic
    – do not read the whole text word by word.

Read these questions first, then look quickly at the text to find the answers. Write short answers, in your own words.

1 Which country is the text about?

2 What dates are mentioned, and what happened on those dates?

3 Which four people are named, and what were their relationships with each other?

4 What did George III suffer from?

5 Where was George IV crowned King?

6 Why did the Prince Regent marry Princess Caroline?

When George IV finally inherited the British throne, he had been waiting a long time for the opportunity to wield power and control his own finances. His father, George III, had suffered from repeated bouts of mental illness (now thought to be caused by a hereditary blood disorder which modern-day drugs could have cured): contemporary treatment for this was so painful that
5   it helped to turn his nervous breakdowns into fits of insanity.

Even while George III was still alive, his son had been declared Prince Regent, in order to rule the country while the King recovered from his madness. But in 1820 George III finally died, and George IV was crowned King in Westminster Abbey, to his great delight.

George IV's wife, Princess Caroline of Brunswick, was not crowned with him, or even allowed
10   to attend the coronation. He had married her in 1795, hoping that Parliament would then pay off his bills and give him a much larger allowance. The marriage was disastrous, however, as the Prince took an instant dislike to her, and did not even receive as much as he had hoped from Parliament. Even when she produced an heir to the throne, Princess Charlotte, the Prince did not relent. He sent Caroline to live in a modest house in Blackheath, south-east London, and only
15   allowed her to visit her daughter once a fortnight. She soon tired of these restrictions, and spent several years travelling around Europe, leading a colourful, adventurous life.

When she heard of the old King's death, Caroline returned immediately to England, to be crowned Queen with her husband. Popular opinion supported her, but the Prince was insistent that she would never be Queen. His attempts to prove that she had been guilty of immoral
20   behaviour succeeded, but he still could not get the divorce he wanted. So Caroline was turned away from the door of Westminster Abbey, with the excuse that she had no ticket for the coronation, and George IV was crowned alone.

Feedback

When you finish a test in this book:

- check your answers in class or with the Key
- read the Feedback section carefully and do the exercises
- work out why you made mistakes, if you made any
- make a note of anything you want to remember.

1 What is the difference between skimming and scanning? Write down what you think, and check with your teacher or the Key.

2 What vocabulary did you find difficult? Write down a synonym or paraphrase for each item in this list, using only the meaning in the text.

a to inherit the throne	f contemporary	k heir
b to wield	g insanity	l relent
c bouts	h Regent	m modest
d hereditary	i coronation	n immoral
e disorder	j allowance	o colourful

☞ **3** Here is some guidance to help you find the answers to questions 1-6 in Progress Test 1, if you found this exercise difficult.

1 *Which country is the text about?*
'British, Westminster Abbey, south-east London'

2 *What dates are mentioned, and what happened on those dates?*
Just run your eye down the page looking for numbers.

3 *Which four people are named, and what were their relationships with each other?*
Just scan the text looking for people's names.

4 *What did George III suffer from?*
Look out for the phrase 'suffer from'.

5 *Where was George IV crowned King?*
Look for place names.

6 *Why did the Prince Regent marry Princess Caroline?*
Look for 'The Prince Regent had married her ... hoping that ... ' and put it in your own words.

As this is the first test in the book, **Progress Test 1** has been made easier than in the actual FCE exam. Most of the events in the text are in chronological order, that is, in the order they actually happened. In the exam, however, and in later tests in this book, you may find that the order of events is not so clear, so you will have to **look for clues** to help you answer the questions.

The clues in this text are the names, the dates and the places (e.g. George IV, 1795, Blackheath). When the order of events is not chronological, or not clear, we often use the past perfect to show what had happened earlier. There are several examples of this in the text – can you find them?

Watch out for **clues** in the next test you do!

Intensive reading with multiple choice

Intensive reading involves a very careful, thorough reading of a text. Underline or highlight words you do not know, and look them up or guess their meaning. Paraphrase difficult groups of words. When you come to the end, read the text again, several times if necessary, until you feel you really understand all of it.

A **multiple choice** exercise offers you a series of statements or questions about the text, with alternative answers. Here are some tips for dealing with this:

- As the text comes first, **read it first, intensively**.
- Cover up the alternatives and look at the statement or question *only*, then find an answer in the text, which you state in your own words. Now look at the alternatives and select the one which is closest to your first answer.
- Eliminate the alternatives that are clearly irrelevant or wrong.
- Be wary of alternatives that are too similar to the text: these are called **distractors**, because they distract you from the right answer.
- Remember that it is what the text says or implies that counts, not your own knowledge or experience.
- If there seems to be more than one right answer, re-read the question and the text carefully. Make sure you are really answering the question.

 A Read this text and answer the questions which follow.

Scheduled and charter flights are almost indistinguishable in terms of seat comfort these days, at least for the Economy passenger. However, the check-in time is much shorter for a scheduled flight, and there is considerably less risk of delay, overbooking and other problems so often associated with the cheaper end of the market. Prices fluctuate according to season, time of day and whether you fly at the weekend or mid-week. Occasionally you can obtain a scheduled flight for the same price as a charter, but normally the price is a good deal higher. On the whole, scheduled flights are booked by business people and those who value reliability above economy, while charter flights are popular with package holidaymakers and individuals on a tight budget.

1 What do these words in the text mean?

A considerably	C fluctuate
B associated	D reliability

2 Paraphrase these phrases.

A are almost indistinguishable	C those who value reliability above economy
B the cheaper end of the market	D on a tight budget

3 What is one advantage of a scheduled flight, according to the text? Answer in your own words.
Now look at these four alternatives and select the one closest to your answer.

A less waiting around before take-off	C less dangerous
B better service by airline staff	D popular with tourists

4 Choose the correct answer.
Scheduled flights are much better than charters

A as they are cheaper.	C for people making economies.
B in terms of seat comfort.	D although they usually cost more.

Which is/are the distractor(s) here?

B Do the same with this text.

Although Brazil has its share of environmental and social problems, it has its successes too. One of these is the town of Curitiba, where the authorities, including the mayor, Jaime Lerner, have shown evidence of a strong vision and commitment to good environmental practice. In the shanty towns there are no flies or litter, because there is a voluntary recycling exchange system. A constant procession of women and children bring rubbish they have collected in bags or on wheelbarrows; for a kilo of litter they are given a kilo of potatoes and one of bananas. This means the streets stay clean, and people do not go hungry.

Public transport is also well organized. The buses are of the latest design, with platforms that open out at the same time as the doors, designed to allow a large number of passengers to board quickly. Tickets are bought beforehand to save time, and the bus travels fast on its own dedicated bus lane. Many motorists now leave their cars at home and take the bus to work, to cut costs and reduce traffic. The people of Curitiba are all involved in protecting their environment.

1 What do these words or phrases in the text mean?

A shanty town   C voluntary
B litter   D to board

2 Paraphrase these phrases.

A have shown evidence of   C a constant procession
B commitment to good   D a dedicated bus lane
    environmental practice

3 Who has/have set up this environmental initiative in Curitiba?

A the mayor, Jaime Lerner   C motorists
B the people of Curitiba   D the town council or local government

4 How does the recycling exchange work?

A Rubbish is paid for.   C Rubbish is exchanged for food.
B Rubbish is sorted and recycled.   D People get rid of their own rubbish.

5 How do the buses avoid getting stuck in traffic jams?

A They are of up to date design.   C People do not pay their fares on the bus.
B Other vehicles are not   D Drivers respect and give way to them.
    allowed to use bus lanes.

Reading between the lines

Sometimes you are not only required to answer questions based on your understanding of the gist and the details of a text, but also to deduce meaning from the context. The answer you want may not be stated in black and white, but will be implicit in the text. Finding this is known as **reading between the lines**.

As you read a text, ask yourself, 'How does the writer feel? What is the atmosphere like? What would I do in this situation?' These are the kinds of questions which need a careful reading of the text and an understanding of its cultural, social and emotional background.

 Read this text carefully and answer the questions which follow.

Liz went into the library, hoping to find Mark. There was something important she wanted to say to him. He was sitting in his usual place, at one of the computers. He didn't look up when she spoke to him.

'Mark ... I ... How are you? Things OK?' She desperately wanted to keep the tone light.

'Liz, hi. Yeah, I guess so. Just gotta get this essay typed out. The Prof's been hassling me for it for two weeks now.'

She sat down in the empty seat next to him and put her hand on his arm. 'Look, Mark, I need to talk to you. We ... we need to talk. Don't we? Don't you agree? Mark, please!' She was beginning to sound upset.

'Gimme a break, Liz. I gotta lot on my plate just now.' His fingers were still playing over the computer keyboard and his eyes stared fixedly at the screen.

She took a few deep breaths. Keep calm, she told herself. He always hated it if she started crying. 'OK, Mark,' she said. 'Shall we go for a coffee after the seminar? It's Tuesday, remember. We could go to the Italian place.'

'No chance, babe,' he said. 'I'm cutting the seminar – need the time to finish this.'

Liz stood up. 'Well, see you around, then.'

'Yeah, catch you later.'

1 What kind of relationship do you think Liz and Mark have?

2 What do you think she wants to talk to him about?

3 Who do you think is more interested in their relationship, Liz or Mark? Why do you think that?

4 From the text, what can you tell about a) Liz's character   b) Mark's character   c) Mark's nationality?

5 What do you think Liz means when she says, 'It's Tuesday, remember'?

6 What does 'catch you later' mean? (Guess if you don't know.)

7 What do you think happens next in the story?

8 Do you sympathize more with Liz, or Mark? Why?

9 Which adjectives from the box would you choose to describe Liz's and Mark's characters or attitudes? Justify your choices.

sympathetic	helpful	selfish	moody	sensitive
emotional	disciplined	passionate	tactful	patient
hardworking	uninterested	flexible	rude	

Read these paragraphs and answer the questions.

At first glance the village looked just the same, but then he realized the pond had been grassed over, and there was a car park where the cricket ground had been. He stood looking at the rows of shiny new cars on the asphalt where runs had been scored and matches won and lost. It seemed a waste, somehow.

1 Had he been there before?

2 Did he prefer it in the past or the present?

Moira's room was on the second floor. There was no heating, and the wind blew under the door and down the chimney in wild, violent gusts. Moira shivered. Would tonight be one of the nights? Would the long-dead Baron make one of his regular appearances? Would he come to claim her as victim number 3? She held her breath and listened. There was a scratching kind of noise outside her door.

3 What do you think has happened so far in the story?

4 Why do you think Moira shivers?

Carole sighed as she put the letter back in the envelope. She knew they would have to go, although John probably wouldn't be keen. He was very busy these days, with his new responsibilities, and looked so tired most of the time. What a pity Edinburgh was so far away, a long way to drive on your own, and anyway her boss certainly wouldn't let her take the time off at the moment. Perhaps later, when the summer rush was over ... She looked at the silver-framed photo on the piano, and smiled reassuringly at the white-haired old lady who was staring out at her. 'It's all right,' she whispered. 'I'll arrange it somehow. We'll be there.'

5 Where is Carole planning to go, and who is she going to visit?

6 What can you find out about the relationship between John and Carole?

7 Which adjectives from the box best describe   a) Carole   b) John   c) neither of them?

> worried   hard-working   enthusiastic
> careful   caring   exhausted

When you start a test in this book, remember to:

- read this study box first to find out what reading skills you need
- read the instructions (the rubric) very carefully
- concentrate hard on doing the test, with no distractions!

The following test is to see how well you can **read intensively, with multiple choice questions**. You may also have to **read between the lines** for some answers (see Units 3 and 4).

Remember – read the text **intensively**
– try to think of your own answer first
– eliminate wrong answers
– answer only according to the text, not your experience
– watch out for distractors!

Read this text carefully and answer the questions which follow. Only one answer (A, B, C or D) is correct.

Cristina Sánchez, Europe's first female matador of modern times, has been training for ten years to become recognized as a Spanish bullfighter. In her teens she fought a small cow in a field and fell in love with bullfighting. She immediately cut short her training as a hairdresser, and attended the professional bullfighters' academy in Madrid, where she was the only woman among more than a hundred men. She graduated in third place, an exceptional result.

Cristina herself accepts that the matador's art is more difficult for a woman than a man, as men are generally taller and stronger, but she maintains that it is possible, if a woman trains hard and is light on her feet. Nevertheless, she has been badly injured in bullfights on several occasions, and does not underestimate the dangers involved.

She is resigned to receiving harsh criticism from the male-dominated world of *la corrida*, but admits she often feels lonely. Holding her own in this macho business is, however, a struggle she is determined to continue, as the sole representative of her sex. 'One day I'll give up,' she says, 'when I decide to start a family.'

1 Cristina Sánchez

A is a recognized bullfighter in Spain.
B is a graduate of the bullfighters' academy.

C fell in love with a bullfighter.
D is Spain's first female matador.

2 According to the text, bullfighting

A is impossible for a woman.
B is equally possible for men and women.

C is all a question of training and physique.
D is only possible for tall, strong men.

3 Cristina

A is used to being criticized.
B accepts criticism happily.

C is mostly criticized by women.
D feels relaxed and happy in her work.

4 She

A is hoping to persuade other women to become matadors.
B is preparing to give up bullfighting soon.

C insists on being taken seriously.
D wants to combine motherhood with bullfighting.

Feedback

When you finish a test in this book:

- check your answers in class or with the Key
- read the Feedback section carefully and do the exercises
- work out why you made mistakes, if you made any
- make a note of anything you want to remember.

1 Which technique did you use? Look back at the study boxes in Units 3 and 4 and decide whether you should have used any of those techniques.

2 What vocabulary did you find difficult? Write down a synonym or paraphrase for each item in this list, using only the meanings in the text.

a matador	e graduated	i macho
b recognized	f is resigned to	j struggle
c cut short	g harsh	k sole
d academy	h la corrida	l start a family

3 Here is some guidance to help you find the answers to questions 1-4 in Progress Test 2, if you found this exercise difficult.

Question 1

A is wrong: she is not yet recognized, 'has been training to become recognized' – the present perfect continuous (here) means the action is not finished yet.
Watch out for the distractors! C and D are wrong: she fell in love with bullfighting, not a bullfighter, and she is the first female matador 'of modern times' (presumably there were others in the past).

Question 2

The meaning of the sentence 'She herself accepts ...' is that it is easier for a man than a woman, but a woman can do it with the right physique/build and training. So A, B and D are all wrong and can be eliminated.

Question 3

You need to understand 'is resigned to'. B is wrong: she accepts criticism but not happily. C is wrong: 'the male-dominated world'. D is wrong: she often feels lonely.

Question 4

A is wrong: she is 'the sole representative of her sex'. B is wrong: she'll give up 'one day', not soon. D is wrong: she will stop bullfighting when she has children.

Like Progress Test 1, **Progress Test 2** is not as difficult as a real FCE reading text. It is shorter, which makes it easier for you to understand, and the ideas are clearly presented, although there is some fairly complicated vocabulary (like *sole* or *macho*). The aim is to increase your confidence by building up the level of difficulty very gradually, and by pointing out possible problems that you may meet in the FCE exam.

It is important to **read and re-read** the questions and the text while ignoring the distractors, until you have found the most appropriate answers. This can take a lot of practice, but you will get used to it!

If you have a long text to skim or scan, you may need to read it fast in order to answer the questions in the allotted time. Here are some ways of improving **the speed of your reading**:

- Do not read each word. You have not got time for this.
- Look at each paragraph, and let your eye travel quickly over it, picking out important words like nouns, verbs, names, dates etc.
- Split the text into **groups of words**, and let your eye travel from one group to another, helped by the linking words.
- Read as much as you can (newspapers, magazines, short stories), just for the **gist**, without paying attention to style, grammar or vocabulary.
- **Time yourself** when reading. How long do you take to read a paragraph, or a page of closely typed print? Aim to reduce the time it takes you to read a particular text.

 Look quickly at this text **for one minute only**. Then cover up the text and write down every word you can remember. You should remember at least some of the words in bold, which will give you the gist of the passage.

Despite the **traffic** which can be **extremely heavy** at times, **Athens** is a most **attractive capital city**, as **tourists** have **discovered** over the years. One of the most **appealing areas** is the **Plaka,** where **picturesque tavernas** rub shoulders with **souvenir shops**, in a patchwork of **nineteenth-century buildings, lanes and squares**. Several **fascinating museums** are housed in **beautifully restored mansions** ...

B Now look at the following text. Which do you think are the most important words for understanding the meaning? Underline, circle or highlight them. You can take your time over this.

Are you a chocoholic? If so, you would probably have felt at home in the ancient Mayan civilisation in Central America. In this sophisticated culture, noted for its outstanding achievements in architecture, astronomy, chronology, painting and pottery, chocolate played a central role, appreciated as a drink and used as a form of currency. Chocolate, which comes from the cacao bean, has been around for at least three thousand years, and has been consumed as a drink for most of that time.

C First read these questions. Then read the text which follows **for three minutes only**, and answer the questions, using short answers.

1 Which country do the islands belong to?

2 What is the food like on Hayman Island?

3 Where did Captain Cook land in 1770?

4 Which is the southernmost island, according to the text?

5 Where would you go for a *quiet* holiday?

6 Which island would you visit for diving?

7 Where is the largest sandy beach in the world, according to the text?

Queensland is home to some of the most magical islands and the largest expanse of coral in the world. It may well be the closest you ever get to paradise. You can while away the hours on a deserted palm-fringed beach, cruise around the coral reef, or throw yourself into the various watersports. Scattered like jewels in the Pacific Ocean, these Australian islands stretch from Lady Elliott in the south to Lizard in the north, and are all a delight to visit.

Hayman, in the Whitsundays, is probably one of the most luxurious resorts in the world, with dreamy beaches, exotic wildlife and mouth-watering cuisine. For something a little more exclusive, try Bedarra, privately owned and with only sixteen villas. For a touch of history, go to Lizard Island, where Captain Cook landed in 1770. This is also where the divers go! To get away from it all, go to Dunk Island, a haven of peace and quiet. Fraser Island has the largest sandy beach in the world, Hook has a wonderful National Park ... The list is endless.

 First read this text **for three minutes only**. Then cover it up and answer the questions which follow.

Gipsies, the Romany-speaking people scattered throughout Europe and North America who maintain their nomadic way of life in our industrialized society, migrated from north-west India from the ninth century onwards. They were first recorded in Britain before 1500, and were originally known as 'Egyptians', as it was assumed they had come from Egypt. (The word *gipsy* derives from *Egyptian*.)

Throughout the centuries there have been many attempts to expel and punish them, and to attack their culture and way of life. Only recently have local authorities been obliged to provide sites for gipsies and other travellers to use as a temporary home. It is true to say that gipsies have suffered severely over the years, but their nomadic lifestyle makes the provision of education and healthcare problematic. There are 90,000 gipsies in Britain today, many of whom do not have access to all the services that might be expected of a civilized society

1 Where did gipsies come from originally, according to the text?

2 When did they first appear in Britain, as far as we know?

3 Where does the name 'gipsy' come from?

4 What is their language called?

5 What are the two main services some gipsies are not receiving?

6 How many gipsies are there in Britain?

If you have a **gapped text** and a choice of clauses, sentences or paragraphs to fill the gaps with, the first step is to get the gist of the text. So, read the title if there is one, and **skim the text for gist**.

When you know what it is about, read it again more carefully, and jot down a word or phrase that might help to fill the gaps.

Next, read the clauses, sentences or paragraphs, and see whether any of them include the word, phrase or idea that you wrote down. If they do, you may have found your answers but, remember, they must make grammatical sense in the text.

A Read this text and choose from sentences A–C the one which fits each gap (1 and 2). Use the clues in brackets to help you. There is one extra sentence.

For most people it is a relatively simple task to buy bunches of fresh herbs from their local supermarket. (1) _____ (*grow them yourself?*)

You can then cut the herbs whenever you want, and add tarragon, chives and marjoram to your soups and casseroles. (2) _____ (*better taste?*)

Just sit back and enjoy the compliments you will receive from your family and friends!

A They will transform the taste of your cooking, and add useful vitamins to your family's diet.

B Occasionally greengrocers can offer higher quality and lower prices.

C Even easier, however, is sowing the seed in pots to keep on your kitchen window-sill.

You need to look for **clues** in order to be sure which clauses or sentences fit. Look carefully at what comes immediately before and after the gap, and try to work out what the topic is. There should be a connection in terms of grammar, vocabulary or punctuation between the main text and the gap-filling sentences.

B Do the same with this text.

I first became interested in classical music when my parents took me to a concert in Vienna. (1) _____ (*how old?*) I can still remember the bright lights, and the beautifully dressed people, and the excitement, and the wonderful, wonderful music. (2) _____ (*connection between then and now?*) I even enjoy practising scales!

A Since then I've learnt to play three instruments.

B I suppose I must have been about four.

C I managed to get hold of a free ticket.

C Do the same with this text.

That winter was the coldest in living memory. Even old Jack Bignall, who was over 90, said so. The schoolchildren were sent home early every afternoon, as the snow continued to fall, and some of the lanes in and around the village became impassable.

(1) _____ (*result of the heavy snowfall?*) All the adults complained bitterly about the snow, but the children loved it.

(2) _____ (*what did the children do?*) Others built snowmen in their gardens, and had snowball fights in the street. The cold snap was over all too quickly for them.

A People enjoyed walking in the bright, clear air.

B When the pond froze over, some of them skated on it.

C For several days there was no postal delivery, and even emergency vehicles couldn't get through.

D Read the text and choose the best clauses or sentences from A-F to fill the gaps (1-5). Use the clues in brackets to help you. There is one more sentence than you need.

A BETTER NIGHT'S SLEEP

Many people complain of sleeping badly at night. There is no single reliable cure for insomnia, but instead of just taking sleeping pills, sufferers should attempt to find the root cause of the problem, and tackle that.

(1) _____ (*what are the causes?*) Worrying about some aspect of your life or work can often prevent you from sleeping. Try to calm your anxieties before you go to bed, and if you wake up with something on your mind, get up and sort it out if you can.

(2) _____ (*cause no. 2?*) All substances containing caffeine can induce sleeplessness, so try to avoid alcohol, coffee, tea etc. too near bedtime. (3) _____ (*other excitement?*)

Finally, a few tips to make sure you are as comfortable as possible. (4) _____ (*an aspect of comfort?*) Keep the bedroom temperature cool: heat will prevent you from sleeping. Read for a while if you find that helpful. Above all, try to maintain a happy frame of mind –

(5) _____ (*start with small letter: if you are unhappy, you'll stay awake*)

If you bear all these points in mind, I am sure you will achieve a healthy, normal sleep pattern in time.

A if you dread going to bed, you will find it more difficult to get to sleep.

B Parties and other late-night activities can also over-stimulate and cause insomnia.

C Another frequent problem is over-excitement of the nervous system.

D Let's look at some of the most common causes of insomnia.

E who have recurring problems getting to sleep.

F Check that your bed does not need replacing; you will probably need to buy a new one every ten years or so.

When you start a test in this book, remember to:

- read this study box first to find out what reading skills you need
- read the instructions (the rubric) very carefully
- concentrate hard on doing the test, with no distractions!

The following test is to see how well you can **complete a gapped text** (see Unit 6).

Remember
- **skim** the text for gist
- re-read it more carefully, looking for **clues**
- write down a word or phrase to fill the gap
- check the sentences or paragraphs to see if any match your ideas.

Read this text and choose from the clauses or sentences A-H the one which fits each gap (1-7). There is one more than you need.

We have known for a long time that diets rich in cholesterol are damaging to health. Throughout the developed countries of the world, people (1) _____ have been cutting down on animal fats, and a low-cholesterol diet is prescribed for anyone in a high-risk category. (2) _____ which, unlike low-fat products, actually brings down cholesterol levels in the body. It is called Benecol, it is made in Finland and, strangely enough, it is a by-product of the forestry industry – that is, it is made from wood. (3) _____ In fact, so high has been the demand for this product that the manufacturers have not been able to keep up with it, (4) _____.

Scientists have been aware for some time that plant sterol, a compound normally discarded as unwanted in the making of wood pulp, can lower blood cholesterol, (5) _____ However, it is only recently that Benecol's Finnish producers, a food and chemicals company, have discovered a way of making plant sterol soluble in fat. This means that it can be consumed in the form of margarine, cooking oil, ice cream or even chocolate – (6) _____ Naturally, this has been an extremely profitable initiative for the company, which hopes to market its product on a worldwide basis, (7) _____

A That fact has not stopped Finnish shoppers going wild about it.

B But now a new substance has been produced

C a very versatile product which will appeal to everyone's taste.

D who are worried about their blood pressure and the risk of heart disease

E when sufficient quantities are available.

F and therefore reduce the risk of heart disease.

G As investors are flocking to buy shares in Benecol,

H and supermarkets sell out of it within hours of a new batch arriving.

Feedback

When you finish a test in this book:

- check your answers in class or with the Key
- read the Feedback section carefully and do the exercises
- work out why you made mistakes, if you made any
- make a note of anything you want to remember.

1 What vocabulary did you find difficult? Write down a synonym or paraphrase for each item in this list, using only the meanings in the text.

a cholesterol	e by-product	i discarded
b throughout	f forestry	j soluble
c prescribed	g going wild about	k consumed
d high-risk	h new batch	l versatile

☞ 2 Here is some guidance to help you find the right clauses or sentences to fill the gaps in Progress Test 3, if you found this exercise difficult.

(1) *'people ... '* Look for a clause starting with a small letter, as this is the middle of a sentence – probably a relative clause starting with 'who' after 'people'. This must refer to people who have heart problems.

(2) You need 'a new product/food/substance' to connect with 'which, unlike low-fat products'.

(3) Look for a new sentence. It obviously talks about how popular the substance is, as the following sentence begins 'In fact, so high has been the demand ...'

(4) Start with a small letter after the comma, and a linking word. Probably this is more about the problems of meeting the high demand

(5) Start with a small letter after the comma, and a linking word. Look for something connected with lowering cholesterol levels.

(6) Start with a small letter after the dash; no linking word is necessary. Look for something connected with eating Benecol in different forms.

(7) Start with a small letter after the comma. Has the company got enough Benecol to sell it round the world, as they keep running out in Finland?

Like Progress Tests 1 and 2, **Progress Test 3** is easier than a real FCE text. You can expect an FCE text to be considerably longer and more complicated, but it is important that you feel confident before you tackle a text at exam level.

This type of exercise involves understanding grammar and punctuation as well as reading skills, and many students find it one of the most difficult, so you may need quite a lot of practice to get used to it. Don't give up if you had difficulty in doing it!

Go back to the test, and **look for clues** (words or punctuation) which point the way to the right answers. Doing that now will help you to find the answers more easily next time.

Source, topic and style

It is often necessary to be able to tell, **at a glance**, where a reading text comes from (its source), what it is about (its topic), and what kind of writing it is (its style). Train yourself to identify the **source, topic** and **style** of a text as quickly as possible, by looking at the headline or title, the level of language, any specialized vocabulary, the punctuation, and whether slang or contractions are used.

Remember that formal writing usually has a higher level of language, with few contractions and no slang, whereas informal writing is normally easier to understand, although it sometimes has broken or disjointed sentences, and colloquialisms as well as contractions.

 A Match each of these short extracts (1-7) with its probable source (A-H). There is one more source than you need.

1 Please come early and wear fancy dress

2 All claims for expenses must be submitted to Accounts with receipts

3 I'm dying to hear how it all goes, so don't keep me in suspense too long! All the best anyway,

4 Melt the sugar and butter together in a saucepan and slowly fold in first the dry ingredients and then the beaten eggs.

5 WANTED — Lift to Keele University this weekend. Can share petrol costs. Contact Pauline on 772672

6 Unfortunately no time today to go to the bank. Kept busy by MB — even worked through my lunch-hour!! Terribly hot all afternoon.

7 It is important to eat a variety of foods in order to maintain a balanced diet. How many different types of vegetables do

A recipe   B notice   C invitation   D letter   E instructions for staff
F diary   G novel   H leaflet on healthy eating

 B Look at these sentences and decide what each one is about. For each sentence, choose the appropriate topic A-K from the box. There is one extra topic. Use each topic only once.

1 Police are hoping the public will come forward with information regarding the violent attack on two teenage boys over the weekend.

2 Some of the highest earning Hollywood stars have got together to record a single which will be sold in aid of the world's poor.

3 The recent wet weather has caused problems for local strawberry farmers, who say their harvest will be badly affected this year.

4 Any supporter found committing acts of vandalism will be banned from future matches, and may be prosecuted.

5 And so it's forty love to Isabella Martinez, thanks to that powerful backhand of hers – it looks as if she's going to win the match!

6 Boiling vegetables for a long time removes the vitamins they contain, and also reduces their taste.

7 He's going to trek overland through India, I think, with a whole group of people – he'll be away for months, of course.

8 I don't suppose there's anything at all on – I haven't seen a good film for years, have you?

9 On Wall Street today the pound fell sharply against the dollar but regained its position by close of trading.

10 You need to slap lots of moisturizer on if you've been out in the sun – it takes a lot out of the skin and really dries it up.

A charity	B punishment	C agriculture	D sport	E money
F beauty	G travel	H food	I crime	J cinema	K radio

C Now look again at A 1-7 and B 1-10, and decide whether you think they are written in formal or informal style. Write F for formal or I for informal for each extract or sentence.

D Read these short texts. What is their source, topic and style (formal or informal?).

1 If fire breaks out, leave the building by the nearest available exit. Do not attempt to extinguish the fire.

2 Sarah —
Josie rang. Will ring back later.
Just off to my Mum's. Remember to put the chicken on!
See you later.
Helen

3 HIS AND HERS – Quality Watches – Only £19.99 the pair including postage and packing. With 2-year guarantee.
Order NOW by phone on 0113-2590078.

4 Please read this booklet before attempting to operate your TV set, which has been manufactured using the most advanced technology available and the most modern production and testing methods.

5 Who's taken my sandwiches? Put them back, or else! Jack

Multiple matching

There are two kinds of **multiple matching** exercises in FCE Paper 1. The first type requires you to match a heading or summary sentence to part of a text, usually a paragraph. To do this you need to:

- Read the headings or summary sentences carefully first, to help you find the appropriate place in the text.
- **Skim** the text quickly for its main points, not the details.
- **Scan** the text for **clues** to help you choose the correct answers. There may be clues in grammar, vocabulary or meaning.
- Watch out for **distractors** (see Unit 3).
- When you have allocated a heading or summary sentence to a particular part of the text, make sure it really sums up its paragraph.

 You are going to read a text about a kind of insect. Read the headings (A–G) and then choose the correct one for each part of the text, using the words in bold to help you. Write the letter in the boxes. There is one extra heading.

A Do's and don'ts B Love it and leave it C Pet problems	
D Disposal E Home sweet home F North and south G A hairy insect	

1

Its Latin name is *Thaumetopoea processionea*, which sounds very impressive, but it's usually known as the processionary caterpillar. It's a small **insect**, only 3–5 cm long, and at one particular stage of its development, its body is covered with an amazing number of microscopic **hairs**, about 600,000 of them! Unfortunately for us, each hair contains a chemical which many humans and animals are allergic to.

2

In the Mediterranean area, it makes a nest at the top of the pine trees, and if you look up, it is easy to see the big fluffy white ball which this caterpillar calls **home**. In the nest, the caterpillar goes through four stages of change, eventually turning into a moth.

3

These insects get their name from the way they walk in a line, one behind the other, and sadly, this is a fascinating sight for most animals. **Cats and dogs**, in particular, are attracted to them, and may sniff the little furry insects, or worse still, try to lick them. Animals' tongues and throats can become severely inflamed because of this, and need immediate veterinary treatment, if serious injury or even death is to be averted.

4

So **make sure** you never walk your dog in a pine forest in Southern France, Italy, Spain or Greece, unless it's on a lead. **Try** to keep cats away from these areas. **Call** your vet at once if your pet has touched one of these caterpillars. **Don't** touch your pet yourself, or you too may experience skin problems.

5

On private land it's the owner's responsibility to **get rid of** these harmful insects, but on public land, it's the job of the local authorities.

6

It's not only the Mediterranean that suffers from this problem. Millions of caterpillars have invaded **Northern** Europe too, and caused damage to thousands of trees.

The second type of **multiple matching** requires you to scan a text for answers to questions, or to match information in the text to statements. To do this, you need to:

- Read the questions or statements carefully first. **Paraphrase** them if you can.
- **Skim** the text quickly for gist.
- **Scan** the text for **clues** to help you choose the correct answers. Names or other vocabulary may help you locate the right paragraph.
- Watch out for **distractors.**
- Make sure your chosen answer really answers the question.

You are going to read some descriptions of TV programmes. Look at these questions and then scan the texts to find the answers. Write the letters A E in the boxes.

Which programme would you watch if you were interested in football? **1**

Which do you think is the most cultural programme? **2**

Which would you watch to find out whether it is going to rain tomorrow? **3**

Which would you watch for pure relaxation and escapism? **4**

Which programmes would be most informative? **5 6 7 8**

A
> *News at Ten* with Alistair Sims.
> *Weather*, Jane Fletcher.   ITV

B
> *The King & the Pirate*
> A drama set in Scotland 100
> years ago. Starring Mel Gibson.
> Movie Channel

C
> *The Big Match Replay*
> Liverpool vs Arsenal.
> Sky Sports

D
> *The Holiday Programme*
> BBC1 Sarah Lloyd investigates
> self-catering in Wales and
> camping on Dartmoor.

E
> *For Art's Sake*   Channel 4
> The new exhibitions at the
> Prado and the Louvre.

F
> *Health Check*   BBC2
> Looking at the nation's health,
> with Andrew McKenna.

When you start a test in this book, remember to:

- read this study box first to find out what reading skills you need
- read the instructions (the rubric) very carefully
- concentrate hard on doing the test, with no distractions!

The following test is to see how well you can scan a text for answers to questions, using **multiple matching**, type 2 (see Unit 8).

Remember – read the questions first
          – **scan** the text for answers, looking for **clues**
          – watch out for distractors!

You are going to read some short texts advertising different products. Read these questions and then choose from products A–H. Write the letters in the boxes.

What would you buy

for displaying a collection of china?	1
for preparing vegetables?	2
for squeezing oranges?	3
for making bread?	4

What would you use

to clean and protect a motorbike?	5
to find out more about a pet?	6
when weeding the garden?	7

A Give your arms a rest with this mains-powered potato peeler, which can peel a kilo of potatoes in 2–4 mins. Easy-to-clean stainless steel blades and a safety switch. £49.95

B This comfortable portable beach chair can be put together in under 60 seconds. The tough canvas material ensures it will last for years. Only £24.95

C Liquid polish used by professionals to achieve that showroom shine on cars, bikes, boats and caravans. Protects against bad weather conditions. Apply at least twice a year for best results. £10.99

D If you're mad about cats, then this is the book for you. It includes sections on cat nutrition and cat psychology. Includes postage and packing. £7.50

E Your hands need protecting when doing those dirty jobs in the garage or garden. Strong gardening gloves with double seams, in three sizes. £5.50 a pair

F Beautiful mahogany-look collector's rack – a series of shelves to show a cherished collection of ornaments to perfection. In kit form for you to assemble. £12.95

G Even if you have never baked bread before, nothing could be easier than adding the basic ingredients to this automatic bread maker, and switching on! It does the rest! Available in two sizes £85/£110

H Squeeze citrus fruit effortlessly with this mini juice extractor. Uses 4 AA batteries (not supplied). £14.95

Feedback

1 Where do you think these mini-texts come from?

   a an instruction leaflet   c a cookery book
   b an in-store booklet   d a mail-order catalogue

2 Why would somebody read them?

3 What vocabulary did you find difficult? Write down a synonym or paraphrase for each item in this list, using only the meaning in the texts.

   a mains-powered   e apply   i cherished
   b peel   f nutrition   j in kit form
   c portable   g seams   k ingredients
   d tough   h mahogany-look   l effortlessly

☞ **4** Here is some guidance to help you find the answers to questions 1–7 in Progress Test 4, if you found this exercise difficult.

   1 *What would you buy for displaying a collection of china?*
      F 'to show ... to perfection' means to display well.

   2 *What would you buy for preparing vegetables?*
      A 'peel a kilo of potatoes' means to prepare potatoes for cooking.

   3 *What would you buy for squeezing oranges?*
      H Oranges are citrus fruit. 'Squeeze' is in the text.

   4 *What would you buy for making bread?*
      G 'baked bread', 'automatic bread-maker'

   5 *What would you use to clean and protect a motorbike?*
      C 'shine on cars, bikes ...' 'Protects against ...'

   6 *What would you use to find out more about a pet?*
      D A cat is a pet, the only animal mentioned in the whole text.

   7 *What would you use when weeding the garden?*
      E 'when doing those dirty jobs in the garden', 'Strong gardening gloves'

5 Would you buy any of these items yourself, or do you think they are unnecessary and a waste of money?

Like the other tests in Section 1, **Progress Test 4** is shorter and easier than a real FCE text. However, it helps to build up your skills by presenting you with FCE-level vocabulary and style. Don't be put off by unfamiliar words or phrases, as you can still answer the questions quickly and correctly even if you don't understand all the vocabulary.

A practical way of understanding this type of text better is to find advertisements in newspapers or magazines, and read them carefully to see what style of writing they use. Then try to write your own advertisement for a tool, gadget or appliance, using similar vocabulary. This will help you to get the hang of the style.

In the next section, you will see how the reading techniques you have practised so far can be used in FCE. So look back at the eight units and four Progress Tests in this section, to make sure you understand them, before going on to **Section 2**.

Good luck!

Headings and summary sentences 1

> **Reading Part 1** of the **Revised FCE** examination involves a **multiple matching** exercise (type 1). There will be a list of headings or summarising sentences, followed by a text with numbered gaps at the beginning of paragraphs. You will be asked to match the heading or sentence with the correct paragraph of the text. There will always be one extra heading or sentence that you will not need. Here are some tips:
>
> • As the headings or sentences come first, read them first, carefully.
> • **Skim** the text for gist.
> • Look at the headings again, decide which topic they refer to, and **scan** the text to see where they would fit in most appropriately.
> • Look for **clues** in the headings and watch out for **distractors**.
> • Use **speed reading**, because you can allow yourself only about 15 minutes for each reading task in the examination.
>
> Look again at the tips in the first study box in **Unit 8, Multiple matching** before you continue with this unit. Write your answers in pencil or on a separate sheet, if you want to do the exercises again later.

 You are going to read part of a leaflet on safety precautions. Choose the most suitable heading from the list A-F for each part of the leaflet. There is one extra heading.

A Further information	D What are the facts?
B What are the danger signs?	E How long to wait
C What to do	F What is it?

BREATHING CAN BE FATAL

> **1**

During an average year about 50 people die from carbon monoxide poisoning in the UK, caused directly by fumes from home heating appliances which are subsequently discovered to be defective. More than 150 people a year are made ill by inhaling the fumes, and have to have hospital treatment. These deaths and illnesses are unnecessary, and can easily be prevented.

> **2**

Carbon monoxide has no colour, smell or taste, and it can kill. It can be given off by any equipment which burns a fossil fuel, for example, coal, gas or oil. Fumes may enter your home if the equipment is faulty, or if the chimney is blocked, or if the room does not allow circulation of fresh air.

> **3**

Watch out for any of the following: gas flames burning orange or yellow (they should be blue), dirty or sooty marks on or above the heater, and wood or coal stoves which burn slowly or go out. You yourself may feel sleepy, or have headaches, chest or stomach pains, sickness or sudden giddiness.

> **4**

If you notice any of the above, stop using the appliance and call a qualified engineer immediately. See your doctor at once if you have physical symptoms. Make sure your heaters are all serviced regularly, have your chimneys swept once a year, and keep air-vents and windows unblocked.

> **5**

If you need more details, you can ring the following numbers:
   Solid Fuel Association – 0800 600 000
   Oil Firing Technical Association – 01737 373311
   Gas Consumers' Council – 0645 060708.

Check your answers in class or with the Key. What mistakes did you make?
Write down the numbers here. _____

What words do you want to remember? Write them down here.

_____

_____

_____

Without looking back at the text, can you explain these words?

precautions _____

fumes _____

appliances _____

defective _____

giddiness _____

solid fuel _____

Now check your answers with the text.

Can you unscramble these words, which come from the study box?

misk _____   *ucles* _____   *spit* _____

stiq ___   *ruislatracs* _____   *lipcen* _____

> **Remember**
> – read the **headings first**, carefully
> – skim the text for gist
> – re-read the headings and scan the text to see where they might fit
> – look for clues
> – use **speed reading**
> – watch out for distractors!

B You are going to read part of a leaflet printed by the local tourist office for visitors to Winchester, a town in the south of England. Choose the sentence A-H which best summarises each part of the leaflet. There is one extra sentence.

A Special group visits can be arranged.

B There are a number of interesting works of art in the cathedral.

C Volunteers are badly needed to show people round.

D There is no charge for visiting the cathedral.

E It is extremely easy to locate the cathedral.

F The cathedral is a solid, ancient building.

G Church services take place daily, at regular times.

H A well-known writer is buried here.

WINCHESTER CATHEDRAL

1

Winchester Cathedral is situated between the railway station and the River Itchen. It is surrounded by attractive gardens, green spaces, and the narrow lanes and half-timbered buildings of this ancient city. It is well signposted, so finding it presents no problems for the visitor.

2

It was built between the eleventh and thirteenth centuries and has stood the test of time well, although the tower was rebuilt in the twelfth century, and work is continually in progress to maintain the fabric of the building and prevent any further decay.

3

Although Winchester may be most famous for its large round painted table, supposed until very recently to be the original Round Table of the legendary King Arthur, a steady stream of visitors come to the cathedral to look at the grave of a writer. Jane Austen, the author of *Pride and Prejudice* and other highly regarded novels, died in 1817 and was buried here.

4

It costs nothing to visit the cathedral, as free access has always been granted to visitors, but we rely on your generosity to help us meet the costs of running the building, currently over £600,000 a year. Please make a donation if you can.

5

You can wander around at your own pace, or you can ask the voluntary guides for help and information. They are easily identified by their red badges. Please note the times of services in the cathedral – 8.00 a.m. and 5.30 p.m. every day – and avoid these times for sightseeing if possible.

> **6**

Don't miss the 12th-century marble font, the 12th-century wall paintings, the 15th-century Great Screen, and the 20th-century sculptures in the Lady Chapel. These are all regarded as important artistic achievements in their own right.

> **7**

If you wish to bring a school group, please contact the Information Desk for details. Advance warning is needed. Educational visits are a feature of the cathedral's contribution to the community.

Check your answers in class or with the Key. What mistakes did you make?

Write down the numbers here._____

What words do you want to remember? Write them down here.

_____

_____

_____

Complete the following phrases by choosing from the words in italics the word which was actually used in the text.

_____ _____ spaces	*open/airy/green*
_____ buildings	*wooden/half-built/half-timbered*
its large round _____ table	*painted/golden/dining*
a _____ stream of visitors	*regular/happy/steady*
_____ access	*free/easy*
a _____ group	*school/students'*
_____ warning	*advance/early*

Now check your answers with the text.

This test is to see how well you can **match headings** with a text.

Remember – read the **headings first**, carefully
– skim the text for **gist**
– look for clues in the headings and the text
– watch out for distractors!

You are going to read a newsletter circulated to a group of residents in a community. Choose the most suitable heading (A-I) for each part of the newsletter. There is one extra heading.

A Mark it and keep it

B Good neighbours

C Late-night action

D Be wary of strangers

E Good news for Whitbridge

F Take your valuables with you

G Call for help if you need it

H A crime-free community

I Keeping burglars away

Canberra Road Neighbourhood Watch Newsletter

1

We had an attendance of just over 20 to hear Sergeant Wilson from Hurley police station give us a very helpful report and update, with a wide-ranging discussion afterwards. He is one of a number of local community specialist officers – with Sergeant Brown at Whitbridge, Sergeant Harris at Walsham, and Sergeant Freeman at Minton as the Safer Community Coordinator. First the good news: there has been NO reported crime in our road this year! In the Whitbridge police area as a whole there were 533 crimes reported this year. For comparison here are the other local area figures: Hurley & Walsham 839, Minton 398; Chartwell 393 and Little Beding 763.

2

So we in Whitbridge live in a safe area, with the consistent problem being simply thefts of, and from, cars. This accounts for almost a quarter (23%) of all the reported crime. The police are addressing this with extra patrols, the use of unmarked cars and surveillance in car parks. The warm weather makes it worse, with car windows left open, and handbags, cameras etc. left in view, but even in winter people are not careful enough. Don't tempt the car thief!

3

The best defence of our homes is simply to fit window locks – and to use them (leaving the key out of sight and not in full view on the window sill). A burglar alarm is a good deterrent but also has to be used sensibly. It is important to ask a neighbour to hold a key and to give the police the name of a keyholder. Automatic floodlighting is another good deterrent, even though most break-ins take place during the day when people are at work or otherwise out. The possibility of extra street lighting will be investigated with the Council.

4

Property marking with stencils or ultra-violet pens is a great help in identifying stolen goods that are recovered. The pens and kits are available cheaply and readily at do-it-yourself shops and stationers. All that is required is to mark the house number and the postcode.

5

When we go away, Neighbourhood Watch comes into its own. Telling the neighbours (and the police, who do keep an eye on things) means that the free newspapers left sticking in the letterbox can be popped in (and remember to cancel the milk and papers anyway). Making the place look lived-in is a great help. The greatest test of neighbourliness might be, in a lengthy absence, to get the grass cut!

6

In all suspicious circumstances, tell the police. By the way, dialling 999 keeps the phone line open automatically, so even if you can't risk speaking – if for example you think someone has broken in and is close by – the call can be quickly traced by the exchange and the police informed.

7

There are occasional trends in door-to-door visits by people who say they are salesmen or researchers. So it is worth watching out. Always ask to see their identification, and if in doubt, do not let them in. Many casual callers are simply enterprising and honest, but others could well be opportunist, with criminal intent.

8

There has been considerable local newspaper coverage of young gangs in the area causing problems. In fact it's probably only about a dozen youths, but the police are active in clamping down on trouble *now*, with foot patrols in our village from 6 pm to 2 am, to nip problems in the bud as far as possible.

Check your answers in class or with the Key. What mistakes did you make?

Write down the numbers here. _____

What words do you want to remember? Write them down here.

_____

_____

_____

Which technique was most useful in the test?_____

What tips would you give another student who is about to start this type of reading task?

_____

_____

_____

Reading Part 2 of the FCE examination consists of a text followed by a number of four-option multiple choice questions. In this case you need to read the text carefully to understand not only the meaning, but also all the details, and you may be required to deduce answers from the context. Here are some tips:

- As the text comes first, **read it first, intensively**. Re-read it if necessary, and guess the meanings of any difficult words.
- Read each question without looking at the alternatives A-D, then look back at the text, and work out the answer yourself according to the text.
- Next read the alternatives A-D and choose the one which is closest to your answer.
- Eliminate the alternatives that are obviously wrong, and watch out for **distractors**.
- Check that you are really answering the question, and that your chosen answer is **stated or implied** in the text.
- Try to **read between the lines** by thinking about the writer's feelings and situation.
- Identify the **source, topic** and **style** of the text (see Unit 7) to help you answer the questions more accurately.
- Allow yourself only about **15 minutes** for this reading task in the examination.

Look again at the tips in the study boxes in **Unit 3, Intensive reading with multiple choice** and **Unit 4, Reading between the lines** before you continue with this unit. Write your answers in pencil or on a separate sheet, if you want to do the exercises again later.

 You are going to read a newspaper advertisement for a competition. For questions or statements 1-6, choose the answer (A, B, C or D) which you think is most appropriate according to the text.

Short Story Competition – £20,000 prize money to be won

The International Writers' Group (IWG), based in San Francisco, is sponsoring an International Open Short Story Competition, with a total of 500 prizes to be awarded over the next twelve months. The closing date for entry is 31 December. Another competition begins on 1 January. The competition is open to all writers, and entry is free.

5 'We are delighted to be extending our sponsorship to Europe this year,' said the President of the IWG, Dorothy Leadbetter. 'Our competitions in the USA have always been extremely successful. It is group policy to make every effort to discover new talent, so we are particularly interested in receiving stories from people who have had nothing published so far, as well as from established authors.'

10 To enter the competition, simply send in one original short story on any subject and in any style to: The International Writers' Group, Dept 4011, FREEPOST, Ipswich, Suffolk, IP2 6SN. Your story should not exceed 3,000 words, and your name and address should appear at the top of the first page. The text should preferably be typed, but a handwritten copy is acceptable, as long as it is legible.

15 All the short stories entered for the competition will also be considered for possible publication in the IWG's collections of short stories, which come out at regular two-yearly intervals. The author of each story chosen for publication retains his or her copyright and is paid royalties on the number of copies sold. The IWG hopes to receive a large number of entries in order to establish this competition as a regular landmark in the arts world. More than 3,000 writers have
20 so far benefited from competitions it has sponsored.

1 This year's short story competition is offering

   A one prize of £20,000.
   B 500 prizes of £20,000.
   C sponsorship to 3,000 writers.
   D £20,000 in prizes.

2 This is the first time the IWG

   A has run a competition in England.
   B has sponsored a short story competition.
   C has asked for entries from unpublished writers.
   D has eliminated the entry fee.

3 If you wish to enter and stand a chance of winning, you should make sure

   A you send your story to the IWG in San Francisco.
   B your story is over 3,000 words.
   C your story is all your own idea.
   D your name and address are on a separate piece of paper.

4 Your story will not be accepted if

   A the competition judges cannot read it.
   B it is written in an unusual style.
   C the subject is considered unsuitable.
   D you have had stories published before.

5 If the judges like your story, it

   A may be published in an annual collection.
   B will earn you a prize and royalties.
   C will be published in two years' time
   D may be published with other authors' work.

6 The IWG is hoping to

   A publish a large number of authors.
   B run this competition again in future.
   C sponsor a two-yearly competition.
   D pay for its prizes out of the entry fee.

Check your answers in class or with the Key. What mistakes did you make?

Write down the numbers here. _____

What words do you want to remember? Write them down here.

_____

_____

_____

> **Remember** – **read the text first, intensively**
> – read each question without looking at the alternatives A-D
> – work out the answer yourself according to the text
> – from the alternatives, choose the one closest to your answer
> – check that you are really answering the question.

 You are going to read a newspaper article about two people. For questions or statements 1-6, choose the answer (A, B, C or D) which you think is most appropriate according to the text.

SIAMESE TWINS

Twin babies born joined together at some point are known as Siamese twins. Although the tendency these days is to operate on the twins, in order to separate them and allow them to lead independent lives, some have lived together for many years without being surgically separated. In fact, the original Siamese twins lived for sixty-three years joined together. They were born in
5 1811 in Siam, the country now known as Thailand, and were called Chang and Eng, meaning 'left' and 'right' in the Thai language. It is because Chang and Eng became so well known during their lifetime that twins born joined together since then have been called Siamese twins.

Chang and Eng shared no organs but were connected by an arm-like tube between their bodies, which did not appear to cause them any problems. As children, they swam in the Mekong river,
10 catching fish for their mother, and were noticed by an English businessman, who realized what a fascinating sight Europeans would find them. He therefore brought them to Europe, and thus the twins' career began.

At that time circuses and travelling shows were extremely popular; people would happily pay to see anything unusual. And when a sea captain, Abel Coffin, took over the twins and brought
15 them to America, their nationwide tours were a sell-out. The twins, however, were anxious to keep their dignity as far as possible, and once they reached adulthood at the age of twenty-one, they took charge of their own affairs, and only allowed themselves to be on show with a certain reluctance and numerous restrictions. People were not permitted to approach and touch them, for example. Their aim was to achieve respectability at all costs.

20 They were not anxious to undergo what was then a complex and dangerous operation to separate them, and seemed content to be joined. Once they had made a considerable sum, they settled in North Carolina in the USA, and lived comfortably there for more than forty years. Unfortunately they were on the losing side in the American Civil War. And when the South surrendered in 1865, they lost their comfortable position and income. So they were obliged to tour the country
25 again, and were on show in other countries around the world.

Over the years Chang's moods had become darker and he had started drinking. On their way back from Russia by sea, he fell ill with lung disease, which eventually killed him, and his brother too, in 1874.

1 Siamese twins

   A are not usually separated these days.
   B are twins who look exactly the same.
   C always share a heart.
   D take their name from a country in Asia.

2 Chang and Eng

   A were the first recorded Siamese twins.
   B were the oldest living Siamese twins.
   C could not swim well.
   D felt uncomfortable together.

3 Why did people pay to see the twins?

    A The twins were part of a circus.
    B It was a sight they were not used to.
    C Coffin was good at publicising shows.
    D Americans especially like twins.

4 Did the twins enjoy being on show?

    A Yes, they made a lot of money.
    B No, they wanted people's respect.
    C Yes, they were used to it.
    D No, they were too young.

5 Why did they go back to touring after 1865?

    A For political reasons.
    B They did not want to fight.
    C They needed the money.
    D They enjoyed it.

6 Eng died

    A when he was 74.
    B because he was a drinker.
    C as a result of his brother's death.
    D when he fell into the sea.

Check your answers in class or with the Key. What mistakes did you make?

Write down the numbers here. _____ _____ _____ _____

What words do you want to remember? Write them down here.

_____

_____

_____

This test is to see how well you can answer **multiple choice** questions about a text.

Remember
- read the **text first, intensively**
- try to **read between the lines**
- check that you are really answering the question
- watch out for distractors!

You are going to read a text about the problems of old people. For questions 1-7, choose the answer (A, B, C or D) which you think fits best according to the text.

Elderly people all over the world are coming out of retirement to earn enough to feed themselves and their families. In the developing countries, the elderly were once protected, and highly regarded as a source of wisdom and folklore; in the highly developed West, those who had worked all their lives used to feel they had at least earned the right to a pension and a
5   comfortable old age. All this is changing, as wars, disasters and disease hit the Third World, and Western governments reduce social security budgets.

In African countries like Kenya and Uganda, young people have moved to towns in large numbers, looking for work, and leaving their grandparents isolated in rural areas. The stresses and strains of modern life are threatening the time-honoured tradition of financial support for
10   elderly family members, and to make matters worse, there will be a huge increase in the proportion of people over sixty in the next few years. Many old people no longer feel needed or respected, and may not even be cared for when they fall ill, as jobs become scarcer and poverty spreads among the working population. In addition, there are many families, particularly in East Africa, trying to cope with the aftermath of AIDS, and it often falls to the grandparents to look
15   after children whose parents have died.

In parts of Eastern Europe, massive political and economic changes in recent years have meant huge price rises for fuel, rent and food. Some pensioners have had to return to work just to pay their bills. The hyperinflation caused by the collapse of the Soviet Union has wiped out many people's savings, and reduced the standard of living considerably for most pensioners. In
20   Western Europe, the elderly find it hard to make ends meet on their state pension, and it is now generally accepted that people will need to make their own pension arrangements in future. From now on, we cannot rely on the social security system to support us when we are old.

1 Why are the elderly taking new jobs?

   A They need money for necessities.
   B They are bored with retirement.
   C They want to be able to afford a few luxuries.
   D They want to pass on their wisdom to others.

2 What was the situation in the past?

   A Old people were expected to work all their lives.
   B Pensions did not allow for a comfortable old age.
   C There was a higher regard for folklore.
   D The elderly felt they were valued members of society.

3 Why are the elderly being neglected in Africa?

   A All traditional customs are being forgotten.
   B People are too poor to look after elderly relatives.
   C Towns are not suitable places for old people.
   D Old people do not give such good advice these days.

4 What additional problem is there in East Africa?

   A The elderly may be victims of AIDS.
   B Whole families may be eliminated by disease.
   C Old people may have to take care of orphans in their family.
   D Grandparents may have no one to look after them.

5 Why are pensioners in Eastern Europe returning to work?

   A They want to be involved in the political and economic changes.
   B They would prefer to pay their bills more promptly.
   C Hyperinflation has caused problems in other countries.
   D Their savings have all gone.

6 What is most likely to happen in future in Western Europe?

   A Governments will raise the social security budget.
   B Families will look after their elderly relatives.
   C Workers will pay into private pension plans.
   D Everybody will economise to make ends meet.

7 What is the general tone of the text?

   A pessimistic
   B humorous
   C unsympathetic
   D hopeful

Check your answers in class or with the Key. What mistakes did you make?

Write down the numbers here. _____ _____

What words do you want to remember? Write them down here.

_____ _____ _____

_____ _____ _____

_____ _____ _____

Which technique was most useful in the test? _____

_____

What tips would you give another student who is about to start this type of reading task?

_____

_____

_____

Gapped texts 1

Reading Part 3 of the FCE examination consists of a text with gaps; the missing sentences or paragraphs, plus an additional one, follow the text, in jumbled order. You are asked to decide where the sentences or paragraphs belong in the text. Here are some tips:

- As the text comes first, **skim** it first, for gist.
- Now **re-read it intensively**, writing down a word or phrase that might help to fill the gap.
- Next, read the sentences or paragraphs, and look for **clues**, which may be similar to what you wrote down; identify the topic.
- Check that the grammar, vocabulary, punctuation and meaning all make sense for your chosen answers.
- Allow yourself only about **15 minutes** for this reading task in the examination.

Look again at the tips in the study boxes in **Unit 6, Completing gapped texts**, before you continue. Write your answers in pencil or on a separate sheet, if you want to do the exercises again later.

 You are going to read part of an article on Edward Jenner. There are six gaps in the text. Choose the most appropriate sentence (A-G) to fit each gap. There is one extra sentence.

JENNER'S CONTRIBUTION TO WORLD HEALTH

Smallpox is an acute, highly infectious disease, producing high fever and a pinkish rash of spots which, when they dry up, leave ugly scars on the skin. **1** It was not until 1980 that the World Health Organization declared that the disease was eradicated, after the final recorded case in Somalia in 1977.

About two hundred years ago the English physician Edward Jenner discovered the process of vaccination, which eventually offered reliable protection and caused smallpox to disappear completely. **2** Here he saw people suffering both from smallpox and from cowpox, a weaker, much less dangerous form of infection, frequently found in cows. He made the interesting observation that the local country people who caught cowpox because of their daily contact with cattle, did not catch smallpox, even if close friends and family were infected. **3** This process was called vaccination, from *vacca*, the Latin word for cow.

Although other studies were being carried out elsewhere in Britain during the eighteenth century, Jenner made the clinical breakthrough, and the immunity he provided against one of history's most terrifying diseases brought him fame and fortune. **4** He was also given the freedom of the City of London in 1805, an honour not lightly granted. He died in 1823.

5 By this time, vaccination had become a compulsory part of many countries'

public health programmes. It may seem surprising that Jenner's great discovery was not fully

exploited at the time. **6**

In the village of Berkeley in Gloucestershire, where Edward Jenner used to live, there is a

museum which aims to remind us of this English physician's pioneering achievement. The lives

of thousands of people have been saved by this one man's careful observation and clinical work.

A This can be partly explained by the fact that complete eradication required a concerted effort from all countries.

B By experimenting on local people, therefore, Edward Jenner was able to prove, in 1796, that injections of the cowpox virus could provide protection against smallpox.

C He was paid generous sums by the British government when the authorities realized the importance of his achievement.

D After a lifetime of hard work, Jenner finally retired to the country, still hoping for the recognition he felt he had earned.

E For centuries it killed rich and poor alike, spreading fast when it took hold in an area, and often seriously disfiguring or blinding those sufferers who escaped death.

F Smallpox was not finally wiped out, however, until almost two centuries later.

G Jenner was born in 1749 and, after studying medicine, lived and worked as a doctor in a small village in rural Gloucestershire.

Check your answers in class or with the Key. What mistakes did you make?

Write down the numbers here. _____

What words do you want to remember? Write them down here.

_____

_____

_____

> **Remember** – **skim** the text
> – **re-read it intensively**
> – look for **clues** in the sentences or paragraphs
> – **check** that your answer makes sense.

B You are going to read an article about a village. Choose the most appropriate sentence (A-H) to fit each gap. There is one extra sentence.

The Village That Vanished

It isn't unusual to hear about a missing person, but in 1930 a whole village vanished – and it's still missing.

1 ☐ Although it was an isolated spot, the Inuit[1] people who lived there were frequently visited by trappers who swapped furs and joined them for meals. **2** ☐

But in November 1930, when Joe decided to stop by the village for a visit, he immediately knew something was wrong. **3** ☐ He shouted a greeting but no one answered. Finally, he opened the doors to several of the huts and yelled for his friends. **4** ☐

An hour-long search of the village showed that every inhabitant had disappeared. There were no signs of a struggle – pots of food sat over fires that had been cold for weeks. **5** ☐ Kayaks had been left unattended for so long that waves had battered them. Rifles stood gathering dust. The Inuits' dogs were found dead from starvation, tied to stumps[2].

The mystery deepened when LaBelle searched his friends' cemetery where bodies were customarily covered with rocks. One grave had been opened and the body exhumed[3]. Stealing a body, LaBelle knew, was taboo for an Inuit. **6** ☐

The Royal Canadian Mounted Police investigated LaBelle's report of the village that disappeared. **7** ☐ Months of detective work, including interviews with other tribes in the area, never turned up a clue to explain the village that vanished.

---

[1] *Inuit:* formerly known as Eskimo
[2] *stumps:* wooden posts
[3] *exhumed:* dug up, removed

A Despite their reputation of 'always getting their man', the Mounties were baffled⁴ as to how and why thirty Inuits, in the middle of winter, had disappeared.

B The first thing was that all the doors were open.

C The village was located near Lake Angikuni, about five hundred miles north-west of the Royal Canadian Mounted Police base at Churchill, Canada.

D A needle was still in some clothing that a woman had been mending.

E First of all, the dogs didn't bark.

F No one replied.

G Whoever had done the deed had stacked the grave stones in two piles – ruling out any possibility that an animal had uncovered the body.

H French-Canadian trapper Joe LaBelle, who had travelled through that part of the Canadian wilderness for about forty years, considered the folks who lived on Lake Angikuni old friends.

⁴ *baffled:* puzzled, mystified

Check your answers in class or with the Key. What mistakes did you make?

Write down the numbers here. _____

What words do you want to remember? Write them down here.

_____ _____

_____ _____

_____ _____

Without looking back at the texts, can you explain these words?

infectious _____ _____

eradication _____ _____

scars _____ _____

immunity _____

Inuit _____

stumps _____ _____

exhume _____

Now check your answers with the texts.

This test is to see how well you can complete **gapped texts**.

Remember
- **skim** the text for gist, then **re-read** it intensively
- jot down a word or phrase that might fill the gap
- look for **clues**
- **check** that your answer makes sense in terms of grammar, vocabulary and punctuation.

You are going to read a text about the writer Dylan Thomas. There are seven gaps. Choose the most appropriate section or paragraph (A-H) to fit each gap. There is one extra one.

DYLAN THOMAS

Dylan Marlais Thomas was born in Swansea in Wales in 1914. His parents had been brought up in the Welsh-speaking countryside and although they taught their son to speak only English, he grew up surrounded by the culture and speech of South Wales, which were to play an important part in his work.

1

He was diagnosed as asthmatic, and because of these problems he was worried about his health all his life, and felt sure he would die young. So his view was that he might as well enjoy life to the full, however short it was going to be; he started chain-smoking at fifteen and later took to drinking heavily.

He had a quite amazing disregard for the practical details of day-to-day life.

2

When he was eight, he started writing poetry, and his work appeared in his school magazine. He showed absolutely no interest in any school subject except English, which he was extremely good at.

3

He got a job as reporter on the *South Wales Daily Post*, but left after fifteen months, and had no further regular salaried employment. Still living at home, he did some acting at the Swansea Little Theatre, for an amateur theatrical company.

4

In 1933 he visited London and made some useful publishing contacts, sending work to various journals. In 1934 he went to live in London and published two books of poems. In 1936 he met his future wife, Caitlin Macnamara, with whom he had a long-lasting, passionate and stormy relationship.

5

He was now becoming famous, and made his first radio broadcast. He became extremely depressed when he failed his medical test and was rejected for active service in World War II. In addition to his worries about his health, he was always short of money, as he seemed to spend it so fast. Then in 1948 there was a disastrous discovery.

6

Partly to economise, Dylan and Caitlin returned to Wales and settled in the village of Laugharne. They had three children by now, and this was the poet's final really productive writing phase, including his radio play *Under Milk Wood*.

7

But exhaustion, illness and drinking took their toll, and on 9th November 1953 Dylan Thomas died, having collapsed a few days earlier.

A This was a very important time for his writing. In those few years of living at home after leaving school, he wrote most of his best-known poems.

B His mother took him to chapel but his father read him Shakespeare instead. For much of his childhood, serious lung problems kept him in bed.

C But critics have only recently come to appreciate the fire and originality of his writing.

D Other people often had to take on his responsibilities. The last years of his life were ruined by ill health and financial difficulties.

E The authorities found out that Dylan Thomas had paid no tax at all during his life and, as a result, he was in debt to the tax office and others right up to his death.

F At last he achieved his ambition of going to America, to give talks and readings around the country, in 1950, 1952 and 1953.

G Neither had any idea about managing money. However, they were deeply in love all their lives, despite the difficulties they had to cope with.

H He left school at sixteen without passing any exams, and was only interested in poetry.

Check your answers in class or with the Key. What mistakes did you make?

Write down the numbers here. _____ _____ _____

What words do you want to remember? Write them down here.

_____ _____ _____ _____

_____ _____ _____ _____

_____ _____ _____ _____

Which technique was most useful in the test?

_____ _____ _____ _____

_____ _____ _____

What tips would you give another student who is about to start this type of reading task?

_____ _____ _____ _____ _____

_____ _____ _____

_____ _____ _____ _____

Locating information 1

Reading Part 4 of the FCE examination involves a **multiple matching** exercise (type 2), where a text must be scanned to provide answers to questions, or to locate information.

- As the questions or statements come first, read them first, carefully.
- **Paraphrase** them if you can.
- **Skim** the text quickly for gist.
- **Scan** the text (see Unit 2) for the appropriate answers, looking for **clues**.
- Do **not** read the text intensively; it would take too long.
- Keep an eye on the time; you can allow yourself **only about 15 minutes** for each exercise in the examination, so use **speed reading** (see Unit 5).
- As you read, identify the **source**, **topic** and **style** of the text (see Unit 7).

Look again at the tips in the second study box in **Unit 8, Multiple matching** before you continue with this unit. Write your answers in pencil or on a separate sheet, if you want to do the exercises again later.

 You are going to read eight short extracts about television programmes. For questions 1-13, choose from extracts A-H. Some of the answers may be chosen more than once. For questions 14 and 15, choose the most appropriate answer from A, B, C or D.

Which programme(s) would you watch

if you were keen on politics?

1	2

if you were interested in health problems?

3	4

if you were involved in international finance?

5	6

if you wanted to watch television on Friday evening?

7	8

if you were planning a holiday?

9

if you wanted to avoid eating meat?

10

if you wanted to keep up to date with scientific research?

11

if you enjoyed programmes on history?

12	13

14 Where would you find these extracts?

    A in a business magazine
    B in a TV guide
    C in a tourist leaflet
    D in a guidebook

15 Which topic is missing from the extracts?

    A medicine
    B the supernatural
    C sport
    D social comment

A TRAVEL SHOW – Thursday 2130
Presenters Jan Fortune and Robbie Michaels go off the beaten track to introduce you to some of the world's most exciting and remote islands. This week – Tuvalu and Pitcairn.

B QUESTIONS IN THE HOUSE – Saturday 2100
The final episode in the drama serial set in the corridors of power. Will the President recover in time to prevent his rivals from overthrowing the government? Will society be able to survive the struggle between right and wrong? "Incredibly close to real life" (*The Herald*); "This could happen to us" (*Daily Observer*).

C THE HISTORY MAN – Sunday 2000
Jacques Baudouin, professor of ancient history at the Sorbonne, Paris, explains the comparative roles of men and women in Ancient Rome, using data from recent archaeological finds near Pompeii to illustrate his ideas. This is one of the lectures by eminent speakers in the *Civilisation* series.

D INTO THE FUTURE – Friday 1830
Jake Mitchell reports on the first medical trials of a new type of cancer therapy in California, and Sophie Murdoch finds out the latest and most scientific way of keeping salmon healthy on fish farms.

E WHAT'S COOKING? – Tuesday 1900
Italian chef Giuseppe Bardolini shows us the secrets of Sicilian cuisine, while Paula Greene investigates vegetarian beliefs and recipes, and gives us ten tips for a low-cholesterol diet.

F NEWS AND WEATHER – Monday to Friday 2100
The latest international news and business bulletins from around the world, with headlines, interviews with political experts, regular feature stories, and global and local weather. Presenters: John Bateman and Cherry Singh.

G THE WAY IT WAS – Monday 2130
Simon Henton visits the royal palace of Versailles, as it used to be in the Sun King's time. An ancient monastery in Sussex, Michelham Priory, yields up its secrets to Maddie Hadley, and Alan Campbell spends a night in Scotland's oldest house, which has a famously visible ghost.

H MONEY MATTERS – Wednesday 1800
A weekly magazine programme covering all aspects of finance and business round the world, including special reports from our correspondents and an analysis of important economic developments.

Check your answers in class or with the Key. What mistakes did you make?

Write down the numbers here. _____

What words do you want to remember? Write them down here.

_____

_____

_____

When doing this type of exercise, why should you read the questions first?

_____

· Why shouldn't you read the text intensively?_____

How long can you allow yourself for this task in the exam?_____

Should you skim or scan the text? _____

Check your answers in the study box.

> **Remember** – read the **questions first**, carefully, then **paraphrase** them
> – **scan** the text for the answers
> – do **not** read the text intensively
> – identify the **source**, **topic** and **style** of the text
> – use **speed reading**.

 You are going to read eight short extracts about books published recently. For questions 1-15, choose from extracts A-H. Some of the answers may be chosen more than once. For questions 16 and 17, choose the most appropriate answer from A, B, C or D.

Which book(s)

tell you more about your health?

1	2

are about crime?

3	4

might give you ideas for your garden?

5	6

could you buy for under £9?

7	8	9

would help you keep up with the news?

10

are fiction?

11	12

is a biography?

13

would be suitable for someone whose English is weak?

14

is not highly recommended?

15

16 Where do you think these extracts are from?

A a booking form
B the back cover of a book
C a newspaper TV guide
D a magazine arts section

17 In what style are the extracts written?

A in an objective, critical way
B in extremely simple language
C with humour
D in formal style

A **The Missing Diamond** *£6.95*   Harriet Rosewall goes in pursuit of the international diamond smugglers who have stolen the most valuable jewel in the world. She doesn't seem to realize how determined they are, and how dangerous things will be for her if she continues her hunt. Luckily she has her faithful assistant, Jeff Banks, to help her. And this time Jeff is literally worth his weight in gold.

B **Have a Heart** *£9.95*   A new book reveals all you need to know about natural ways to relieve high blood pressure and reduce the risk of heart disease. It describes the lifestyle factors that may be making you vulnerable to a life-threatening illness, and gives you a number of techniques to combat them. Exercises and herbal medicines are also recommended.

C The Complete Guide to Your Body *£14.95*   This hard-backed book describes the workings of the human body in great detail, with colour illustrations. It's invaluable for reference when you have a minor ailment, and is also a self-help manual for keeping healthy, without having to make frequent visits to the doctor. "A most helpful, comprehensive work." *Dr E. Sims, British Medical Association*

D Gardens Galore! *£10.99*   Jackie Hargreaves, the TV gardening expert, visits thirty gardens round the country, from castles to cottages, and gives us detailed plans and plant lists for each one. She recommends plants for chalk and sand, for sun and shade, for North and South, for wet and dry soils, along with her trademark sketches, which readers are sure to find enjoyable.

E A Guide to South America *£8.50*   By far the worst of the bunch this week, this travel book makes miserable reading. Its information on public transport is inaccurate and its maps are poorly drawn. You would do better without it. But it does have some good recommendations for cheap hotels and restaurants.

F Portrait of the Artist *£18.50*   A beautifully produced coffee-table book with many glossy colour photos, this describes the life of the painter Claude Monet, concentrating in particular on his life at Giverny, where he lived from 1883 right up to his death in 1926. There are many fascinating sketches and illustrations of his garden there, which he filled with rare plants, and views of the lake and waterlilies, which he painted so often.

G Pride and Prejudice *£2.50*   Jane Austen's great novel is now available in a shorter form, with the language adapted to a vocabulary limit of 2500 words. Suitable for young readers and foreign learners, it evokes all the atmosphere of Austen's country house society, while being much more accessible. Other adaptations are planned in the same series.

H World Events *£9.95*   This is a round-up of all the most important happenings in the last year, from a global viewpoint. Disasters, wars, epidemics, political events, assassinations, massacres – they are all there, with highly sophisticated comment from experts on how and why they happened. A useful section of the book deals with comparative statistics of crimes committed in twenty countries, as well as population and voting figures.

Check your answers in class or with the Key. What mistakes did you make?

Write down the numbers here.   ____   ____   ____   ____

What words do you want to remember? Write them down here.

_____

_____

_____

Delete whichever of the following options you feel is not appropriate:

   In this type of exercise the text must be *skimmed/scanned* for the answers.

   You *have to/don't have to* read every word of the text.

   You need to read the text *fast/slowly*.

Check your answers in the study box.

This test is to see how well you can **scan a text** for answers to questions.

Remember – read the **questions first**, then **paraphrase** them
– **scan** the text for answers
– use **speed reading**.

You are going to read eight extracts from newspaper advertisements. For questions 1-13, choose from extracts A-H. Some of the answers may be chosen more than once. For questions 14 and 15, choose the most appropriate answer from A, B, C or D.

Which holiday(s)

would cost you less than £300?

| 1 |

would probably be most tiring physically?

| 2 |

offers you the chance to learn a skill?

| 3 |

are in places untouched by tourism?

| 4 | 5 |

involve travelling by coach?

| 6 | 7 |

Which extract(s)

warns about possible lack of comfort?

| 8 |

mention historic buildings?

| 9 | 10 | 11 |

mention camping?

| 12 | 13 |

14 Which do you think is the most appropriate heading for this section of the newspaper?

A Accommodation Abroad
B European Holidays
C Bikes and Beaches
D Going Away

15 Which factor do all the extracts have in common?

A a careful description of accommodation
B exact details of the package price
C a direct, yet persuasive style
D an exclamation or question

A *Departing every Sunday till October 6, from £489*
You are invited to experience the breathtaking beauty of Ireland on board one of our luxury coaches. Here is your chance to take in some of the wonderful West Coast scenery on a relaxing 8-day holiday. You will enjoy the unique atmosphere and traditional, slow pace of life which make Ireland so popular with holidaymakers of all ages.

B *A 2-week journey of discovery for the true traveller*
Travel with us in small groups in overland vehicles to explore the ancient country of Ethiopia. Visit royal palaces, island monasteries, mediaeval churches and rural villages. As mass tourism

has not yet come to Ethiopia, accommodation will be simple and road conditions may be poor. £2185 including air fares, full board.

C *Prague to Venice by bike, £560 including air fare and 13 nights' camping*
It's about 800 miles from the Czech capital to Venice, and I did it in a fortnight, with 130 other cyclists. We rode through southern Bohemia, the Austrian mountains, a corner of Slovenia and part of the north Italian plain, our luggage and tents carried for us in two large vans. Food was served by a mobile catering team. Beautiful views, excellent organisation. Why don't you try it?

D *The real Crete, from £465 per person for 2 weeks including flights*
Giorgos runs the local taverna in the village of Megala Chorafia in north-west Crete. The rustic charm of the area has not yet been spoilt by an invasion of tourists, and you can relax by the sea or in the mountains, enjoying the local hospitality and attractive scenery.

E *Exploring the Coromandel area, return fare London to New Zealand about £800*
Do you want natural beauty, scenic reserves and bush walks? Do you want sandy beaches, clean water to bathe in and plenty of camp sites? Do you want to explore abandoned gold mines, go fishing or birdwatching? If you've answered yes to any of these, you should come to the Coromandel in New Zealand, where camping costs around £5 a night per person and motel rooms are available for £30 (double).

F *London to the Taj Mahal, 7 nights from £950*
Take advantage of our experience in the travel field and join our trip from London by air to Agra, the beautiful 17th-century Taj Mahal, Old and New Delhi, and Jaipur. All hotels are 5-star, and you will be accompanied by our expert guides. Optional excursions include visits to the Bharatpur bird sanctuary and national park.

G *Highland House Party departing 25 May, 6 days from only £219*
A super holiday in beautiful Scotland. All this is included: travel by luxury coach, 5 nights half board, daily excursions to lakes, old castles, and craft centres. Enjoy the whole range of Scottish entertainment, historic buildings and stunning scenery!

H *A coastal paradise, return fare £440 before August*
When you've been round Disney World in Orlando with the kids, what is there left to do? Plenty! Enjoy the fabulous beaches and chance to relax that Florida offers! Learn to sail at one of the sailing schools, go diving, take photos of the amazing mix of modern architectural styles, and taste the glorious variety of seafood, fruit and vegetables on offer in the bustling markets and restaurants.

Check your answers in class or with the Key. What mistakes did you make?
Write down the numbers here. _____

What words do you want to remember? Write them down here.

_____

_____

Which technique was most useful in the test? _____

_____

What tips would you give another student who is about to start this type of reading task?

_____

_____

Look back at the other **Check your answers** boxes in Section 2, and revise the vocabulary you wrote down. Rub out your answers and do the exercises again. Then check that you haven't made the same mistakes!

Now go on to **Section 3**. Good luck!

Headings and summary sentences 2

In **Section 3** of this book, the texts are much closer to the length and level of difficulty you will find at FCE. Each unit is graded, so that the easier or shorter text always comes first.

These texts are all authentic or derived from authentic material, to give you exposure to the everyday English of articles, leaflets, guidebooks etc.

Here are some reminders of how to **match headings or summary sentences** with a text:
- Read the headings or sentences first, to help you find the appropriate place in the text.
- **Skim** the text for gist.
- **Scan** the text to see where the headings or sentences might fit.
- Look for **clues** in grammar, vocabulary or meaning.
- Watch out for **distractors**.
- Use **speed reading**.
- Make sure the heading or summary sentence you have chosen really sums up its paragraph.

 You are going to read a newspaper article about children's exposure to television. Choose from the list (A-H) the sentence which best sums up each part (1-7) of the article. There is one extra sentence.

A There can be later educational problems for children whose early language development is poor.

B Television is sometimes used as a way of occupying children and keeping them quiet.

C Research shows that watching television can seriously affect young children's language development.

D Television can prevent children of all backgrounds from learning to talk well.

E There is educational value in watching certain television programmes.

F Parents can easily help their children to make progress.

G Children often prefer watching television to playing with toys.

H Television viewing should be strictly limited or banned completely for very young children.

TV EXPOSURE DAMAGES CHILDREN'S SPEECH

by Sarah Boseley

1

Too much television is stunting[1] the language development of middle-class children as well as those from deprived inner-city areas, according to a leading speech therapist.

2

Dr Sally Ward, who is considered the country's leading authority on the speech development of young children, believes babies under one year old should not watch television or videos at all. Children of two or three should watch for no more than an hour a day.

3

Dr Ward's 10-year study of babies and toddlers in inner-city Manchester showed television was a very important factor in delaying the speech development of the one in five children found to have problems. The background noise from televisions stopped them learning to talk as early as they should. At eight months, they neither recognized their names nor basic words like "juice" and "bricks". At three, they had the language of two-year-olds.

4

Now she has found that children from well-to-do families at her London clinic are being handicapped in the same way. "The television is being used as a babysitter, with nannies particularly. Some of these middle-class children are spending far too much time watching television and videos.

5

They get very fixed on the colours and flashing lights. They are riveted[2] by the screen. We found in our study it was quite difficult to get them interested in toys."

6

All the evidence showed, said Dr Ward, that children whose language was below standard at the age of three could be set back for life. "They are likely to be educational failures and failures in all sorts of ways. They will go to school with depressed language levels and their whole educational progress is held back."

7

In her Manchester study, Dr Ward found that parents who were taught to turn off the television and talk to their children could quickly repair the damage. Babies of nine months would be back on course within four months.

[1] *stunting:* holding back
[2] *riveted:* fascinated

B You are going to read part of a newspaper article on consumerism. Choose the most suitable heading from the list (A-H) for each part (1-7) of the article. There is one extra heading.

> A Giving up jobs to work for others
>
> B A popular, fast-growing trend
>
> C Making time for music
>
> D Green and proud of it
>
> E Family time
>
> F Missing out, or a better life?
>
> G Teaching traditional principles
>
> H Successful stress reduction

VOLUNTEERS FOR A LEISURE AMERICA

Consumerism? Who needs it? **Walter Schwarz** on a growing trend of people opting for cheerful austerity.

Lynn Kidder had two jobs – computer programming and teaching the piano. She and her husband earned $2,700 a month, but they were too busy to be happy. Lynn wanted to play her piano, not teach it. So they took a course in Voluntary Simplicity (VS). They learned how to cut their spending and enhance their savings. After four years of VS, they achieved Crossover Point (CP); they gave up all their jobs and joined the new leisured class.

Another couple had reached the height of luxurious living in their late thirties. They had a new Audi 5000, a new Jeep Cherokee and a boat on the lake, and went skiing abroad every year, but "felt insecure and unfulfilled". So they signed up for the same course that Lynn went to — the New Road Map Foundation, which teaches VS and FI (financial independence) in nine punishing steps. Now they, too, have left their jobs, live in a small house on the interest from their $300,000 nest-egg – less than a third of the income they had before — and do only voluntary work.

Arnie Anfinson is a lithe and agile 78-year-old who spends much of his time on the Internet and e-mail, networking VS. He was a meteorologist with United Airlines until he sold his house to his daughter and rented back the ground floor. Then he began to live cheerfully on less than $300 a month. Outside the back door he breeds worms for his garden, feeding them with kitchen waste. His clothes are second-hand. "My emphasis is not on saving money but spending responsibly for the environment. I eat to live."

4

The newly leisured call themselves downshifters. Nobody knows how many they are, or whether insecurity, stress or ecological concern is their main motive. But Lynn Kidder is sure the movement is "spreading wildly, recognised as a smarter way to live. You make space in your life for what you really care about. How you do it is up to you."

5

In a big, comfortable, simple house in suburban Seattle, Joe Dominguez runs the New Road Map Foundation with his star ex-pupil, Vicki Robin. Dominguez has become the downsizers' guru. More than 3,000 had taken his course on Transforming Your Relationship with Money And Achieving Financial Independence before he and Vicki published *Your Money Or Your Life*. Dominguez was a Wall Street stock analyst until he retired at 30 to teach others to follow him. "It struck a chord in all sorts of people – from yuppies to people on welfare — who felt they weren't managing money or getting value for things. After all, these are old American values: good use of money, good bargains, and lack of show."

6

He found mothers were the first to see that $10 earned wasn't worth an hour less with their children. "Even little kids learned that an hour more with Mom was worth giving up $10-worth of gadgets."

7

Downsizers have a more demanding intention of living with balance in order to find a life of greater purpose, fulfilment and satisfaction. Charlene MacMahon wrote in Seattle's *Simple Living* Newsletter, "When you simplify your life you do fewer (or none) of the things you don't like to do and more of the things you enjoy. And you seek out only those people and relationships which enhance your life. This is not about deprivation – this is about choices."

Here are some reminders of how to answer **multiple choice** questions about a text:

- Read the text first, intensively. Re-read it if necessary, guessing any difficult words.
- Read each question **without looking at the alternatives** A-D, then look back at the text and work out the answer yourself.
- Next read the alternatives and choose the one closest to your answer.
- Eliminate obviously wrong answers and watch out for **distractors**.
- Try to **read between the lines**.
- Check that you are really answering the question, and that your chosen answer is **stated or implied** in the text.
- Identify the **source, topic** and **style** of the text.
- Allow yourself only about **15 minutes** for this reading task in the examination.

 You are going to read an extract from *My Early Life* by Winston Churchill. Choose the most appropriate answers (A, B, C or D) to the questions.

My brother and I were sent this summer by our parents for a so-called walking-tour of Switzerland, with a tutor. I need hardly say we travelled by train so far as the money lasted. The tutor and I climbed mountains. We climbed the Wetterhorn and Monte Rosa. The spectacle of the sunrise striking the peaks of the Bernese Oberland is a marvel of light and colour
5 unsurpassed in my experience. I longed to climb the Matterhorn, but this was not only too expensive but held by the tutor to be too dangerous. All this prudence, however, might easily have been upset by an incident which happened to me in the lake of Lausanne. I record this incident that it may be a warning to others.

I went for a row with another boy a little younger than myself. When we were more than a mile
10 from the shore, we decided to have a swim, pulled off our clothes, jumped into the water and swam about in great delight. When we had had enough, the boat was perhaps one hundred yards away. A breeze had begun to stir the waters. The boat had a small red awning over its stern seats. This awning acted as a sail by catching the breeze. As we swam towards the boat, it drifted farther off. After this had happened several times we had perhaps halved the distance.
15 But meanwhile the breeze was freshening and we both, especially my companion, began to be tired.

Up to this point no idea of danger had crossed my mind. The sun played upon the sparkling blue waters; the wonderful panorama of mountains and valleys, the gay hotels and villas still smiled. But now I saw Death as near as I believe I have ever seen him. He was swimming in the water
20 at our side, whispering from time to time in the rising wind which continued to carry the boat away from us at about the same speed we could swim. No help was near. Unaided, we could never reach the shore.

I was not only an easy, but a fast swimmer, having represented my House at Harrow* when our team defeated all comers. I now swam for life. Twice I reached within a yard of the boat and
25 each time a gust carried it just beyond my reach; but by a supreme effort I caught hold of its side in the nick of time before a still stronger gust bulged the red awning again. I scrambled in, and rowed back for my companion who, though tired, had not apparently realised the dull yellow glare of mortal peril that had so suddenly played around us. I said nothing to the tutor about this serious experience; but I have never forgotten it.

* *Harrow:* a famous school in England

1 Why was it a 'so-called' walking-tour?

   A The tutor walked, while the writer and his brother went by train.
   B They were supposed to be travelling by train, not on foot.
   C They only walked when they ran out of money.
   D It was a climbing-trip rather than a walking-tour.

2 Why did the writer not climb the Matterhorn?

   A He was not allowed to.
   B He thought it would take too long.
   C Although it would not have cost much, it was considered dangerous.
   D His parents could not afford the expense.

3 Why is the writer telling us this anecdote?

   A to show how cautious he was
   B to describe his holiday in Lausanne
   C to explain how his character developed
   D to prevent others from running the same risk

4 What did the two boys do on the lake?

   A They rowed all round the lake.
   B They dived into the water in their swimsuits.
   C Having rowed the boat some way out, they bathed in the lake.
   D They sailed out to the middle of the lake for a swim.

5 What mistake did the boys make?

   A They did not realize the boat's awning would catch the breeze.
   B They did not know the lake had a strong current.
   C They had no idea they had swum so far from the boat.
   D Neither of them were aware of any danger.

6 Who or what does 'He' refer to in line 19?

   A the other boy
   B a ghost
   C Death
   D the tutor

7 Which of the statements below is true?

   A The boys would not have been able to swim to land.
   B The writer found it easy to reach the boat.
   C The boat was drifting towards him.
   D The other boy was exhausted and frightened.

8 How did the writer react to this experience?

   A He thought it was a trivial, unimportant incident.
   B He was afraid his parents might be angry.
   C He felt proud of saving his friend's life.
   D It made him aware of some of life's dangers.

B You are going to read part of a magazine article about a conservation charity called the National Trust. Choose the most appropriate answers (A, B, C or D) to the questions.

THE NATIONAL TRUST

In 1896 the National Trust paid £10 for its first purchased property, a 14th-century house in East Sussex. And the rest, as they say, is history.

Today the National Trust owns more than 590,500 acres of land and protects another 79,500 acres. That's 1.6 per cent of the land in England, Wales and Northern Ireland (Scotland has its
5 own separate National Trust). The Trust owns holiday cottages, tearooms and restaurants, as well as castles, hamlets and villages. It runs a theatre company, an art foundation and various employment training programmes. It publishes handbooks, magazines, a glossy annual report and a mail-order catalogue that features bone-china mugs, silk scarves and crystal perfume bottles. It has a gift shop in Japan and an American affiliate called the Royal Oak Foundation. It
10 has 2,800 permanent staff, 28,000 volunteers and 2,250,000 members.

In the early 1960s the Trust commissioned a survey to evaluate the opportunities for conservation along the coast of England, Wales and Northern Ireland. Out of more than 3,000 miles of coastline, the Trust judged a thousand to be neither beautiful nor interesting; another thousand, cluttered with marinas, trailer parks, hotels and factories, to be ruined beyond
15 redemption; and the remaining shoreline – of which the Trust already owned 200 miles – to be of outstanding beauty and worthy of protection. In 1965 the Trust launched Enterprise Neptune to acquire these segments.

"We're a nation of seafarers and an island nation, so the very nature of the project motivates people," says Richard Offen, the energetic manager of the Enterprise Neptune appeal. "There is
20 no place in England that is farther than 70 miles from the coast, and everybody has fond memories of seaside holidays as a child. Contributors see themselves as preserving their memories."

St. Michael's Mount, a castle perched on an island hill, looms a few hundred yards off the Cornish coast. Since an abbot first built a small church on the site in 1135, the mount has served
25 as a military outpost, a priory and a residence. After 1659 it became the home of the St. Aubyn family; today it is the home of John St. Aubyn and his wife, Susan, known more formally as Lord and Lady St. Levan.

In 1954 they gave the mount to the National Trust, which ensured that the place would never be sold or tastelessly exploited. In return, the Trust leases the family 16 rooms (out of more than
30 120 in the castle) as well as one of the gardens. The family's lease with the Trust extends for a thousand years. "It is," Lord St. Levan told me with a sheepish grin, "a very happy arrangement."

1 When did the National Trust buy its first property?

A in the 14th century
B in the 19th century
C in the 20th century
D in 1869

2 What does the National Trust own?

A most of the land in Britain
B more than 600,000 acres of land
C a small percentage of Northern Ireland, England and Wales
D some land in England and some in Scotland

3 Which of the following is **not** true about the National Trust?

A It runs cultural and commercial operations in the UK.
B It sells presents and souvenirs in Japan.
C It rents out self-catering accommodation to tourists.
D It owns factories producing pottery, glassware and silk scarves.

4 What was the conclusion reached by the Trust after its 1960s survey?

A About 800 miles of coastline should be bought and protected.
B All British coasts were judged to be of outstanding beauty.
C Marinas, trailer parks and so on should all be removed.
D The 3000 miles of coastline could not all be surveyed.

5 Which of these statements is true, according to the text?

A Nowhere in England is less than 70 miles from the coast.
B The Enterprise Neptune project aims to provide seaside holidays for children.
C The British enjoy their beach holidays and want the coastline to be protected.
D Many supporters of Enterprise Neptune are elderly sailors.

6 What can you discover about St. Michael's Mount from the text?

A The castle was built in 1135.
B It was bought by the Trust in 1954.
C It has been used for religious, domestic and military purposes.
D It has been in the hands of the present owners for more than 300 years.

7 How do you think Lord and Lady St. Levan now feel about the leasing of their home from the Trust?

A proud to have their home on show to the public
B disappointed that they could not keep more rooms
C glad to have made a short-term arrangement
D relieved that they no longer have the problem of running the castle

Here are some reminders of how to complete **gapped texts**:

- As the text comes first, **skim it first**, for gist.
- Now **re-read** the text **intensively**, writing down a word or phrase that might help to fill the gap.
- Next, read the sentences or paragraphs, and look for **clues**, which may be similar to what you wrote down; identify the **topic**.
- Check that your chosen answers make sense in terms of grammar, vocabulary, punctuation and meaning.
- Allow yourself only about **15 minutes** for this reading task in the examination.

Look back at **Unit 6** to read about this kind of exercise in more detail.

 You are going to read an information leaflet for drivers. There are seven gaps in the text. Choose the most appropriate sentences (A-H) to fill the gaps. There is one extra sentence.

The M25 Motorway

Drivers intending to use the M25 Motorway in Surrey need to remember that there are roadworks in both directions between Junctions 6 and 10 (the Godstone to Wisley section).

1 [_____] A compulsory 50 mph speed limit has been imposed throughout the whole length of the roadworks, and motorists who exceed this limit will be prosecuted. **2** [_____] The speed limit is necessary in order to keep traffic running smoothly and safely through the roadworks. In addition, the workforce needs to be protected, and this cannot reliably be done without a 50 mph limit.

There will usually be three lanes open in the daytime in each direction, but at night certain lanes will be closed to traffic. **3** [_____] Calls are charged at normal rates.

The roadworks have been undertaken to add extra lanes in each direction between Junctions 6 and 10, one of the busiest stretches of the motorway. This is being done to aid traffic flow at peak times and to reduce accidents. New road signs and lighting systems are also being installed, to improve road safety. However, we are very conscious of the impact a motorway can have on local residents, on the environment, and on wildlife habitats. **4** [_____]

Please note that the emergency telephones will not be operating on this stretch, and that there will therefore be a free recovery service throughout the roadworks, in order to keep the traffic lanes clear. **5** [_____] A breakdown truck will arrive to tow you to the nearest garage, free of charge.

Here is some advice for the motorist on this section of the M25:

- Allow plenty of time for your journey and avoid the area in the rush hour if you can.

- Keep to the speed limit to avoid the risk of prosecution.

- [6]

- Get into the correct lane in good time and follow the direction signs.

- [7] There may be delays caused by traffic build-up, so you might prefer to travel by train.

You can find out more about the progress of the roadworks by tuning in to BBC Radio or local radio stations, or by consulting Ceefax or Teletext. We hope you will not be greatly inconvenienced, and we ask for your full co-operation.

A Information is available on this line from 7 a.m. to 11 p.m. only.

B Ring 0171 928 5100 for information on train routes and timetables (calls are charged at normal rates).

C As a result, every effort is being made to minimise any negative effects, with the provision of noise barriers, grassy slopes and natural vegetation.

D This particular section is undergoing widening work and improvements to the surface, which started in May and will continue till the end of the year.

E Drive extra carefully through the roadworks and keep your distance from all other vehicles.

F For details of lane closures, drivers can phone 01932 569596 at any time.

G So if you break down, do not set off on foot to try to find a phone, but stay in your vehicle and turn on your hazard lights.

H In order to catch offenders, police speed checks, using speed cameras, will be in operation.

B   You are going to read a text about Vincent Van Gogh, with seven gaps. Choose the most appropriate paragraphs (A-H) to fit the gaps. There is one extra paragraph.

VINCENT VAN GOGH

One of the world's best-known painters, Vincent Van Gogh, was born in Brabant, Holland, in 1853.

| 1 |

He began his working life in 1869 as an employee of the Goupil Art Gallery, where his brother Theo also worked for a time. Vincent stayed with the gallery for seven years, working at branches in The Hague, London and Paris.

| 2 |

From December 1878 to July 1879 he went to a coal-mining district in Belgium as a priest. It was on his return from this post to his native country that he gave himself the task of perfecting his drawing, but he also worked with watercolour and finally in oils.

| 3 |

His subjects, ordinary working men and women, were portrayed sympathetically and without exaggeration. 'The Potato Eaters', painted in 1885, is a famous work dating from this period. Later, in the mental hospital at St Rémy, Van Gogh remembered it with affection.

| 4 |

For three months (December 1885 to February 1886) Van Gogh was in Antwerp, where his artistic development continued. He became more interested in colour, influenced not only by the paintings of Rubens on show in the museums, but also by the Japanese prints he had begun to collect. It was here that he started his cycle of self-portraits.

| 5 |

But in February 1888 he left Paris for Arles, in the south of France, hoping to find the strong light and bright colour which other artists had talked so much about. He soon abandoned Impressionism and concentrated on evolving his own distinctive style.

| 6 |

During his remaining eighteen months of life, he was in and out of hospital, but continued to produce many fully developed works, some of which are now considered masterpieces.

| 7 |

Illness and loneliness had made his life too hard to bear, but he left behind him an impressive legacy of creative artistic achievement.

A However, it was when he moved to Paris in February 1886 that he met other artists and experimented with a form of Impressionism. His works of this period are full of light and feeling, marked by lively brush-strokes and fresh colours, mostly whites, pinks and blues.

B His final few months were spent in the home of a Dr Gachet, who took him in and cared for him. But in the end, fearing another breakdown, Van Gogh put an end to his existence by shooting himself.

C Although he showed a talent for drawing from the age of nine, he did not become aware of his artistic vocation until 1880, at the relatively late age of 27.

D 'I have tried to make it clear,' he wrote, 'how these people, eating their potatoes under the lamplight, have dug the earth with those very hands they put in the dish; and so the painting speaks of manual labour and how they have honestly earned their food.'

E In 1877 he started an apprenticeship in a bookshop at Dordrecht, while at the same time studying theology.

F The French painter Paul Gauguin came to Arles at Van Gogh's invitation, but Vincent's first experience of communal artistic life ended with a crisis, when Van Gogh tried to attack Gauguin, then cut off part of his own ear. The first signs of his subsequent illness had become apparent and, from this moment on, Van Gogh suffered from fits of insanity.

G Known as the Dutch period, this residence in Holland produced works depicting misery and despair. These reflected his experiences in the coal-mining area, when he had been continually surrounded by poverty and unhappiness.

H Surrounded by friends and close family right up to the end, Van Gogh passed peacefully away, after a lifetime of struggle and effort.

Here are some reminders of how to do this kind of **multiple matching** exercise, where you have to **locate information** in a text:

- **Read the questions or statements first**, carefully.
- **Paraphrase** them if necessary.
- **Skim** the text quickly for gist.
- **Scan** the text for the appropriate answers, looking for **clues**.
- **Don't** waste time reading the text intensively.
- Identify the **source, topic** and **style** of the text as you read.
- Use **speed reading**, as you can allow yourself only about **15 minutes** for this exercise in the exam.

 You are going to read part of a magazine article on different families' attitudes to eating. Answer questions 1-14 by choosing from the families A-E. Any of the families may be chosen more than once.

FAMILIES	
A The Thompsons	D The Burke-Johnsons
B The Colleys	E The Sutcliffs
C The Davises	

Which statement refers to which family?

They have changed their eating habits.	1 2
They refuse to eat meat on principle.	3
Their approach to food is traditional and based on routine.	4
They pay little attention to their food.	5
They take care to eat a lot of fresh vegetables.	6
They are proud of their cooking.	7 8
Their lifestyle dictates the way they eat.	9 10
They are worried about eating certain types of food.	11 12
They have happy memories of childhood food.	13
They usually eat separately.	14

FOOD, FOOD, GLORIOUS FOOD!

What are your views on food? How important is it to you? How much time do you spend thinking about it, planning menus, talking about it, preparing it and eating it? Here's what some of you think.

Sarah and Richard Thompson eat only additive-free food that they cook at home. They've been doing this ever since their son Hugo was born. 'We didn't care what we ate before that,' admits Sarah. 'We used to eat all kinds of rubbish, junk food, take-aways, frozen food ... But when you have a child you really become aware of how important food is. We believe you are what you eat, and who'd want to be a hamburger! It does take more time, of course, to do the shopping and prepare everything yourself. We buy fresh fish or meat, and organic fruit and vegetables every other day, and I do a lot of baking. But it's very satisfying to know we're eating the right things, and everything tastes so much better.'

Peggy and Bill Colley are retired now, and Bill does the cooking, as Peggy is in a wheelchair. 'We don't eat as much as we used to,' he says. 'Neither of us has much appetite these days. I remember the Sunday lunch we used to have as kids – all of us round the big table, with huge plates piled high with chicken and veg and roast potatoes, and then a pudding to follow. Oh, it was lovely, but I couldn't manage that now. No, Peggy and I often have cheese on toast, or a bit of soup, or something out of a tin. I'm not much of a cook really. It's too much bother to peel a lot of vegetables, anyway.'

Roger and Caroline Davis both have high-flying jobs and lead a hectic life. 'I can't remember the last time we ate at home together,' says Roger. 'I usually have a meeting or something else on, so I tend to grab a bite to eat in a handy bistro near the office. It's often a working meal, so I hardly notice what I'm eating. It could be pasta or a bit of salad, or occasionally a steak. And Caroline travels a lot for her job, so she's not often at home. She's not really bothered about her food either.'

Trevor and Sue Burke-Johnson have both been vegetarians since their student days, and their children are too. They say there are lots of reasons why they don't eat meat. 'One thing is, we don't have complete confidence in modern methods of food production. Just how safe is meat these days? It could be full of hormones or other additives, which might affect our health. And then another thing is, what right have we got to take over so much of the planet for producing meat? Growing cereal takes up much less space, and developing countries manage very well with hardly any meat at all. Anyway, I couldn't bring myself to kill an animal, so I don't think I should expect anyone else to. I don't think we'll ever eat meat again.'

Henry Sutcliff takes a rather different view. He lives with his two middle-aged sisters, **Betty and Kate**, in the family home. He believes in eating meat every day. 'What was good enough for our parents is good enough for us. We all need protein, don't we? And I maintain you need three meals a day, just to keep going. A cooked breakfast is important, too. You get tired and run-down if you don't eat properly. We really enjoy our food. My sisters do the cooking between them. They use good old-fashioned recipes, and I promise you, their cooking is wonderful!'

B You are going to read some information about the Empire State Building. Choose the correct answers (A-F) to questions 1-19. Any of the answers may be chosen more than once. For question 20, select the best answer from A, B, C or D.

Which section(s) of the text describe(s)

the material the lobby is made of? | 1 |

the night-time view from the top? | 2 |

the building's modern works of art? | 3 |

the outside of the building? | 4 |

In which section(s) do you discover

who designed the building? | 5 |

how high it is? | 6 |

where you can buy something to eat? | 7 |

how famous it is around the world? | 8 9 10 |

Which sections mention

the views? | 11 12 13 14 |

the building's beauty? | 15 16 |

the fact that it can easily be identified? | 17 18 19 |

20 From the texts, it appears that most visitors to the building are

A disappointed.
B respectful.
C hungry.
D impressed.

New York's World Famous Empire State Building ...
"the cathedral of the skies"

A New York's world famous Empire State Building, which soars more than a quarter of a mile into the atmosphere above the heart of Manhattan, has been called "the cathedral of the skies" by many of those who have been awed by the view from the top of The Building.

An internationally known landmark in itself, the commanding position of the most famous building ever erected by man – 1,454 feet (443 meters) – offers inspiring views around the horizon, night or day, in wet weather or dry, to visitors from around the world.

More than 79 million people have marvelled at the breathtaking sights they have beheld from the two observatories, on the 86th and the 102nd floors.

B The 86th floor observatory, 1,050 feet (320 meters), reached by high speed, automatic elevators, has both a glass-enclosed area, which is heated in winter and cooled in summer, and spacious outdoor promenades on all four sides of The Building. High-powered binoculars are available on the promenades for the convenience of visitors at a minimal cost. A snack bar and souvenir counters are also located in the 86th floor observatory.

Standing on the 102nd floor – 1,250 feet (381 meters) above the bustling streets below – one is reminded of the song, "On a Clear Day You Can See Forever". Actually, on clear days visitors can see the surrounding countryside for distances up to 80 miles, looking into the neighboring states of New Jersey, Pennsylvania, Connecticut and Massachusetts, as well as New York.

C The Eight Wonders of the World, the eight original art works in the lobby of The Empire State Building which were created by artist Roy Sparkia and his wife Renee Nemorov, have been a distinguished attraction in the lobby since their unveiling in 1963. Using a technique which permits the artist to paint with light as well as color, the subjects include the Seven Wonders of the Ancient World, as well as the Eighth Wonder of the Modern World – The Empire State Building.

D The lobby of the world's most famous building is a work of art in itself. The marble in the lofty lobby came from Italy, France, Belgium and Germany. Experts combed these countries to get the most beautiful marble and, in one case, removed the contents of an entire quarry to ensure the right color and graining.

E Designed by the internationally famous firm of architects, Shreve, Lamb & Harmon Associates, P.C. of New York City, and completed in 1931, The Empire State Building is "an architectural splendor" which overlooks many architecturally significant buildings in Manhattan.

The exterior of the world's most famous building is made of Indiana limestone and granite trimmed with mullions of sparkling stainless steel which reach from the sixth floor to the pinnacle of The Building. Whether seen in sunlight or moonlight, the tower glistens magnificently.

From the top of the internationally famous landmark, one can take an unsurpassed visual tour of New York City. Centrally located in the heart of Manhattan, it presents unprecedented views to all four sides, North, East, South and West.

F The incomparable night view from the top of The Empire State Building is a fantasy of lights and stars sparkling and dancing against a panoramic background of darkness.

The upper 30 floors of the Empire State Building are illuminated nightly from sunset to midnight either in white or an appropriate color scheme commemorating special events. The Empire State Building dominates the New York skyline both night and day.

SECTION 4   EXAM PRACTICE

Practice Test 1

Part 1

You are going to read an extract from a book 'The Seven Wonders of the Ancient World'. Choose from the list (A-H) the sentence which best summarises each part (1-7) of the extract. There is one extra sentence which you do not need to use.

A Class and economic differences are apparent in the Ancient Egyptians' approach to death.

B These structures serve as the final resting-place of kings.

C Its design is symbolic.

D The Great Pyramid is the largest and oldest stone building in the world.

E Nourishing the spirit was considered important for life after death.

F The achievement of the builders seems incredible to us, reliant as we are on modern machinery.

G It is so old that it appears almost indestructible.

H Special security precautions were taken when burying a 'divine' royal.

The Great Pyramid at Giza

1

The only one of the Seven Wonders of the Ancient World that still exists is also the oldest of them all. The Great Pyramid at Giza in Egypt was built some time around 2560 BC; it was already two thousand years old when work began on the next Wonder, the Hanging Gardens of Babylon. The age of the Great Pyramid – more than 4500 years – is so great that it seems almost as if it has been there for ever, and that it will last for ever. In the words of the Arab proverb, 'Man fears Time, but Time fears the Pyramids.'

2

But age is only one of the reasons why the Great Pyramid is so extraordinary. Another is its size: it is by far the largest of the Seven Wonders and, except for frontier walls such as the Great Wall of China, it is the largest single thing made of stone that has ever been built. Then, too, there is the amazing effort and skill that were needed to cut all that stone and put it together into what is a near-perfect geometrical form, with only simple tools and technology. In fact, if we were asked today for a list of Seven Wonders, ancient or modern, the Great Pyramid would certainly still be on it. But, we may ask, why was such an extraordinary thing ever built? What exactly is it?

3

The Great Pyramid, like the other larger pyramids in Egypt, is the burial place, or tomb, of one of the country's ancient kings. During the period in Egyptian history known as the Old Kingdom (3100-2180 BC), more than twenty pyramids were built at different places along the River Nile. Three of the larger ones are at Giza, which is now a suburb of Cairo. Like all the other pyramids, they are on the west bank of the Nile, with only the desert and the setting sun beyond. To the ancient Egyptians, the west was the home of the dead. This was where the sun-god Ra, who sailed across the sky in his boat during the day, began his nightly journey down through the Underworld.

4

For a person's spirit to survive death, the Egyptians believed that the body had to be preserved. This was because the spirit of the dead person left the body at night, but had to return to it in the morning for food and rest. Without these things, the soul would be lost. Members of a family, or their priests, would therefore place food in the tomb of a dead relative, together with furniture and the other necessities of life.

5

So that the returning spirit would recognize its home, the body had to be kept as life-like as possible, which is why the Egyptians perfected the art of embalming bodies to produce what we now call mummies. We do not know what the ordinary people, who could not afford to pay for embalming, thought would happen to their spirits after their bodies had decayed. Perhaps they simply accepted that, in death as in life, they would not be as lucky as their rulers.

6

Their king, or pharaoh, was considered to be a god – a son, in fact, of the sun-god Ra – and his body had to be especially well protected after death. We can therefore understand why the pyramid which was his royal tomb was so large: by placing the mummy of the dead pharaoh deep inside such a huge structure, the builders thought that no one would ever be able to disturb it.

7

The shape of the structure was important too. a pyramid represented the rays of the sun as they spread out and touched the earth.

Part 2

You are going to read part of a magazine article about Judi Dench. For questions 8-15, choose the correct answer (A, B, C or D).

My dressing room at the National Theatre is a sort of second home at the moment. Michael [Williams] and I live in an old farmhouse on the Surrey/Sussex border, but my day has been very London-based recently, rehearsing *As Time Goes By* for television in Acton and then going on to the National in the afternoons to prepare for my role as Desiree in Sondheim's *A Little Night*
5 *Music*.

It's a small room, but I've got my own bathroom and I've covered the walls with good luck cards and family photos. The window looks out on to a courtyard and all the other dressing rooms, so if you're nosey like me you can catch up on what everybody else is doing.

As Time Goes By rehearsals start at ten, which means leaving home at eight, so I'm up at seven to
10 feed our four cats, the swans, the ducks and the moorhens. We've got a large garden pond and our daughter, Finty, gave Michael four new ducks for his sixtieth birthday last year – Fred and Ginger and Sextus and Zero. I'll just have a boiled egg and a bit of ham and take Mike a cup of tea before setting off for London.

The working day always starts with a cup of decaff – I'd go up the wall if I drank too much real
15 coffee. The team are wonderful and have all become proper friends. This is our fifth series and probably the last. I shall miss them terribly.

Lunch is a bit of fish or chicken in the canteen. I'm careful about my diet because if I eat a bun it immediately comes up on my thigh! If I'm at the National that night I'll go straight across to the South Bank to spend the afternoon going through my TV lines for the next day. I'm quite good at
20 line learning – I can remember the whole of *Twelfth Night* and *A Midsummer Night's Dream*.

After the show I'll have a bath and drive back to the country, arriving home at about midnight and taking in a great gulp of fresh air. Mike often stays up (I always ask him not to) and Finty is sometimes there, too, though she lives in our cottage in Hampstead and we won't be seeing so much of her soon because she opens in a play in London this month.

25 Sundays have recently been taken up with recording *As Time Goes By*, but Michael and I often do a weekend charity recital together – we're connected to 150 charities and I'm no good at making speeches. I love being in my sixties, but I'm always glad when New Year is over. I get frightened looking ahead. I take life as it comes and try to look for the pluses. It's not a bad kind of philosophy.

8 What work are both Judi Dench and her daughter engaged in?

    A acting in stage plays
    B directing television programmes
    C modelling clothes
    D making theatrical costumes

9 What does Judi see as a disadvantage of her dressing room?

    A There isn't a good view from the window.
    B The room could be larger.
    C There are cards and photos all over the walls.
    D She doesn't have to share a bathroom.

10 Where do she and her husband live most of the time?

   A an old farmhouse in Acton
   B her dressing room at the National Theatre
   C a house in the country
   D a cottage in Hampstead

11 What would happen if she 'drank too much real coffee' (line 14)?

   A Her temperature would rise.
   B She'd be nervous.
   C She'd start acting strangely.
   D She'd get used to it.

12 How does she feel about food?

   A She doesn't like cakes or biscuits.
   B She would like to try more vegetarian food.
   C She only eats organic meat.
   D She watches calories because she puts on weight easily.

13 What does she do in the afternoons?

   A She often has a bath.
   B She sometimes sees her daughter.
   C She frequently watches television.
   D She usually learns her part for the next day's filming.

14 What do she and her husband often do at weekends?

   A act together to raise money for people in need
   B make films together for charity
   C record a television series at the studio
   D make political speeches

15 What would you say her attitude to life is?

   A She enjoys planning for the future.
   B She always expects the worst.
   C She has a realistic and positive approach.
   D She enjoys life but is sometimes disappointed with the way things turn out.

Part 3

You are going to read some advice on walking or climbing in wintry conditions. Seven sentences have been removed from the text. Choose from sentences A-H the one which fits each gap (16-22). There is one extra sentence which you do not need to use.

WINTER WARNING

Few people know more about walking than Countrywide Holidays, whose guesthouses include group walking programmes throughout the year. ⬚16⬚

"Walking in the cold, short days of winter is a different world from the warm, long days of summer, especially in the mountains. ⬚17⬚ Walking through a warm, sunny valley is very misleading as you ascend onto the mountains. In winter this is exaggerated, for a slight breeze over snowcapped hills has a drastic chill factor, whilst sun reflecting off snow can be blinding. Conditions can deteriorate within minutes to blow arctic blizzards over the mountain tops, requiring winter clothing, precise navigation and a realistic awareness of the potential dangers.

You will see how quickly blowing snow can cover the tracks of other walkers, and mist can easily hide cairns[1] and waymarks. ⬚18⬚ In this potentially dangerous situation, the use of winter equipment may be required, or diversions made to your route. And bear in mind that the careful use of winter equipment such as ice axes and crampons or having to find an alternative route may hinder progress and take time.

⬚19⬚ It eats into your energy. To cope with the cold the body burns up huge amounts of reserves. Energy is also required in greater quantities to keep walking in snow and against strong winds. ⬚20⬚ This can easily result in an accident. In addition, hot drinks and high energy food are vital, as well as being a great comfort on a cold mountain.

⬚21⬚ Favourite walks completed easily in summer conditions may have to be rushed or cut short for winter days. Changes in conditions, patches of ice or streams in flood can delay walkers, who may become benighted[2]. Thick cloud, mist and dark skies can draw darkness in even earlier.

Some people find winter walking the very best there is – but it demands a greater respect and knowledge of the mountains and increased preparation and fitness. ⬚22⬚ Take extra clothing, food, hot drinks, survival bag, torch and winter equipment which you should already know how to use. Leave full details of your route, escape route and ETA[3], and if in doubt go with an experienced guide."

¹ *cairns:* piles of stones as landmarks
² *benighted:* overtaken by darkness
³ *ETA:* expected time of arrival

A Dusk comes early on winter days and can catch out many an unwary walker.

B So check local weather forecasts, plan ahead within your capabilities and plan alternative routes in case of early descent.

C Tiredness and fatigue are the eventual result of the increased effort.

D Cold is a killer.

E Your route can become perilous, with ice hidden under fresh snow.

F Don't forget to tell someone where you are planning to go.

G Whether you're planning a ramble on the North Yorks Moors or Lakeland fells, the following advice from CH is based on a century of walking experience.

H Remember that weather conditions are always variable in the hills.

Part 4

You are going to read part of a magazine article about people's opinions on education. Answer questions 23-35 by choosing from the people A-E. Any of the people may be chosen more than once.

> A Sharon Woolford
>
> B Simon Taggart
>
> C Emma Rees-Baker
>
> D Robert Wagstaff
>
> E Geraldine Bickerton

Which person implies or states the following opinion?

Practice rather than theory is the best way of learning.

23

Testing students is best done by means of written exams.

24

Modern technology can be a problem for uneducated people.

25

The main aim of education is to help students find a job.

26	27

Teachers should encourage personal development.

28

Pupils and students suffer from the pressure of examinations.

29

The majority of undergraduates could do with some financial help.

30

Acquiring general knowledge is pointless.

31

Teachers should be treated with politeness and consideration.

32

Discipline is an important part of school life.

33

The purpose of education is to ensure that students attain
certain levels of ability.

34

There are more educational opportunities now than in the past.

35

THE HAPPIEST DAYS OF YOUR LIFE?

So what do *you* think education's all about? Let's hear your views! Here are some of our readers' comments so far.

Sharon Woolford left school at 16 because she just wanted to earn some money. Now she's a waitress. Does she regret leaving early? 'No, I don't. I think schools should prepare you for work, and mine didn't. We spent all our time on projects, and learning useless facts. It seemed such a waste of time somehow. Who wants to know what the longest river in Europe is? *I* don't!'

Simon Taggart is a solicitor, and says he worked hard at school because he knew he wanted to get somewhere. 'I passed all my exams, got into university and qualified as a solicitor. People say exams are stressful – well, they are, but I think they're necessary. They're the only reliable way of finding out how good students are at their subjects. And that's what education's all about, assessing a student's potential and performance, and helping him or her to reach high standards of achievement.'

Emma Rees-Baker is a secondary teacher, so she knows what she's talking about. 'It seems to me we should be looking for talent in everybody, trying to discover what that person is about, helping him or her to develop as a creative, thinking individual. So in my classes (I teach art), we do spend some time on theory, but really, practical work is far more important. And that means that tests and exams have to be practically based too. Actually I believe pupils studying *any* subject learn best by doing practical tasks, but I suppose it's easier to see the point with art. I mean, you wouldn't be much good as an artist if you knew the theory off by heart but couldn't produce a painting, would you?! But don't think all this means there's chaos in my classroom. I also believe teachers must maintain control at all times.'

Robert Wagstaff has been studying computer engineering at university for the last two years. He says the media give the wrong impression of student life. 'It's not that easy being a student. Older people often seem to think we're living in the lap of luxury, all at the expense of the taxpayer! Well, I can tell you, nothing could be further from the truth. Most students I know live in pretty bad conditions, and have difficulty getting by on their grant or allowance. And most of us study really hard, sometimes all night. You have to, to be able to hand in your projects and assignments on time. Otherwise you get thrown out of university. So you need to discipline yourself, which is a lot more difficult than someone telling you what to do. Occasionally I ask myself why I'm doing it, but I know the reason. I want a really good, solid job – well, that's the point of all this studying, isn't it?'

Finally, **Geraldine Bickerton** has something to say. 'It's very important to have a good education. And by that I mean being taught the three R's, as we used to say, Reading, Writing and Arithmetic, when you're young. And children should learn proper respect for their elders and betters, especially the teacher. Far too many of these young people simply don't understand that they'll never get anywhere if they don't study and learn things. Life these days is getting more and more complicated – I mean, I can't record a programme on my video without my granddaughter's help – and if they haven't had a decent education, they just won't be able able to cope. Youngsters today are so lucky – they have all these schools and colleges to choose from. They should make the most of it. *My* generation never had the choice.'

Part 1

You are going to read part of a newspaper article on tipping. Choose from the list (A-H) the sentence which best sums up each part (1-7) of the article. There is one extra sentence.

A Undergraduates often work as waiters in order to continue or finish their studies.

B Tipping is a problem for customers, who don't know how much to give.

C Certain qualities are necessary for this type of work.

D There is considerable international variation in tipping habits.

E Customers can be surprisingly aggressive towards a waiter or waitress.

F Doing this job is more demanding than it used to be.

G Despite the difficulties involved, working as a waiter in the right restaurant can be lucrative.

H A waiter or waitress may have low social status.

WAITING GAME IS STRICTLY FOR PROS[1]

*The British are mean when it comes to tipping, writes **Jane Headon***

1

In the United States, waiting at tables is more a profession than a job. Wages are token and staff expect to live off their tips. The more professional the service given, the more lucrative the reward. During a bout of postgraduate travel, I waited at tables in New York and at one Wall Street restaurant; I was disappointed if my tips didn't exceed $400 a week. In Britain, the experience tells a different tale. Money and respect are handed out in more carefully guarded measures to those who serve food.

2

Yet lack of respect hasn't stopped students from taking waiting jobs to eke out a steadily shrinking grant. Nicola Sizer is 28 and finishing a four-year teaching degree at Goldsmiths University. A £2,000 debt at the end of her first year forced her into waitressing at the Village Taverna, a Greek restaurant in south-east London. She is paid £10 for a session which lasts from 6 p.m. until after midnight. Most of her money comes from tips. On a good night, she'll make £30 ($45); on a poor one, she'll be lucky to scrape £15. "Some nights people come in and don't leave you anything," she says. "People forget that the waitress isn't there to have a good time."

3

Chris Pye waited at tables at five London restaurants over a three-year period. He worked for a short time at Pasta Mania where, as in many restaurants, the official policy was that waiters paid for 'runners' (customers who leave without paying). "I'd been waiting on a really nice couple for about an hour and been having a good time with them," he recalls. "I turned my back for a couple of minutes and, when I turned back, they'd gone." Outraged[2], Pye followed them across Soho, where he was rewarded by a punch in the face. "It amazed me that two such apparently respectable people could abuse me in a way that they would never abuse their local shopkeeper."

4

Dave Turnbull, district officer for the hotel and catering section of the Transport and General Workers' Union, admits there are particular problems with tipping. "It depends on what form the tips are," he says. "Also, there's nothing legal to say that the service charge goes to the waiter." But he concedes that working at the right place can be financially very rewarding. Central London has the highest concentration of restaurants in the country. If there is serious money to be made anywhere, it is here.

5

Jane Stocks is 34 and has been waitressing for five years. She's been at the Chicago Pizza Pie Factory in Central London for one year. Waitressing is her career choice – she enjoys the social aspect of the work and the fact that her opinion counts. Outside, she doesn't always get treated so well. "If I'm going to look for an apartment and I say that I'm a waitress, people say 'Oh'," she says. "When applying for a credit card or a bank account, waitressing isn't the kind of job that they respect."

6

Not everybody can handle waitressing. Gina Clough, aged 26, manages the Chicago Pizza Pie Factory and says countless waitresses have left in tears. "People know a lot more about food these days and they expect more," she says. "Going out for a meal used to be a perk[3]. Nowadays anybody can go out for food. It's a hard job waitressing. At the end of the day, if the customer's not happy, you're the one to blame."

7

Although Clough can point to waitresses earning tips of £100 on a good night, she is firmly of the opinion that it's not a job anybody can do. Stocks agrees: "You've got to be able to take a lot of responsibility, a lot of stress and concentrate on a lot of things for a long time. You've also got to be all different things to all people."

---

[1] *pros:* professionals
[2] *outraged:* shocked and angry
[3] *perk:* treat, fringe benefit

Part 2

You are going to read an extract from *Adventures in Two Worlds* by A.J. Cronin. For questions 8-14 choose the most appropriate answer (A, B, C or D).

Having emphatically declared before my entire household that I *would* write a novel – tacitly implying, of course, that it was the fault of every other member of the household that I had not written twenty novels – I found myself faced with the unpleasant necessity of justifying my rash remarks. All I could do was to retire, with a show of courage and deep purpose, to the top attic of
5 the house, which had been at once selected as 'the room for Daddy to write in'. Here I was confronted by a square pine table, by a pile of twopenny exercise books, and a dictionary.

It was the morning following our arrival. Amazingly, for that latitude, the sun shone. Our little dinghy danced entrancingly at anchor on the loch, waiting to be rowed. My car stood in the garage, waiting to be driven. The trout in the river lay head to tail, waiting to be caught. The hills stood
10 fresh and green, waiting to be climbed. And I – I stood at the window of the little upstairs room. Wincingly, I looked at the sun, the loch, the boat, the car, the river and the mountains; then sadly turned and sat down before my pine table, my exercise books and my dictionary. 'What a fool you are,' I said to myself gloomily. How often during the next three months was I to repeat the assertion – each time with stronger adjectives.

15 But in the meantime I was going to begin. Firmly I opened the first exercise book, firmly I jogged my fountain pen out of its habitual inertia. Firmly I poised that pen and lifted my head for inspiration.

It was a pleasant view through that narrow window: a long green field ran down to a bay of the loch. I thought I might contemplate the scene for a minute or two before settling down to work. I
20 contemplated. Then somebody knocked at the door and said, 'Lunchtime.' I started, and searched hopefully for my glorious beginning, only to find that the exercise book still retained its blank virginity.

I rose and went downstairs, and I carved the mutton glumly. My two young sons, removed by their nurse to a remote distance in order that they might on no account disturb the novelist, had
25 returned in high spirits. The younger, aged four, now lisped breezily: 'Finished your book yet, Daddy?' The elder, always of a corrective tendency, affirmed with the superior wisdom of his two additional years: 'Don't be silly. Daddy's only half finished.' Whereupon their mother smiled upon them reprovingly: 'No, dears, Daddy can only have written a chapter or two.'

8 Why did the writer have to start writing a novel?

   A He was competing with the other writers in his family.
   B He was in need of money.
   C He wanted to show everybody how brave and purposeful he could be.
   D He had told his family he would write one.

9 How did he feel when he stood at the attic window?

   A eager to get on with his work
   B depressed at the thought of the task ahead of him
   C annoyed with the weather
   D exhilarated by the beautiful countryside

10 What happened during the morning?

   A He wrote the beginning of the novel.
   B He settled down quickly to his writing.
   C He looked at the view through the window.
   D He wrote the first chapter, then lost it.

11 What does 'I started' mean in line 20?

    A I began to write at once.
    B I looked fixedly at the paper in front of me.
    C I immediately began to look for my first chapter.
    D I jumped, in surprise.

12 What did his wife and sons think about his writing?

    A He must be making good progress.
    B He should have finished the book already.
    C It was a pity he had to spend so much time writing.
    D It was fortunate he was able to write fast.

13 How would you describe the writer's character?

    A boastful, too interested in himself
    B cheerful, sociable
    C determined, hard-working, a perfectionist
    D aware of his faults

14 What would a good title for this text be?

    A A family holiday
    B Pressure to write
    C Three months of effort
    D Self-improvement

Part 3

You are going to read a newspaper article about an old sailor. Seven paragraphs have been removed. Choose the most appropriate paragraph (A-H) to fit each gap (15-21). There is one extra paragraph.

AMAZING LIFE OF THE OLD MAN OF THE SEA

One of the great seafaring eccentrics, Tristan Jones, has died at 71.

15

He never had much money, recognition or fame, but Tristan Jones has been called the greatest lone sailor of our age.

16

For a year and a day he was trapped in the ice. Yet he got within 285 miles of the record. The voyage took two years and the book he wrote about it, *Ice,* is a classic.

Tristan Jones sailed 400,000 miles, mostly alone, and held dozens of records. He was born at sea, on his father's ship as it rounded Cape Horn.

17

He went to sea when he was 14 and was sunk three times before his nineteenth birthday. During the war he served as a stoker on the battleship Warspite, rising to petty officer three times but each time being demoted to stoker – 'for fighting', he said.

18

The Arctic voyage, funded by his £3-a-week Navy pension, was only the beginning. Afterwards, desperate for money, he went back to stoking boilers – this time in Harrods, where he lived off scraps from the food hall. As soon as he had half enough for a boat, he was off again.

19

As well as going round the world, he held the record for the greatest vertical voyage – from the Dead Sea in Israel, 1,310 ft below sea level, to Lake Titicaca in the Peruvian Andes, the world's highest lake at 12,506 ft.

20

Frequently his journeys were halted by poverty: he would hole up in a port, write another book, and on the proceeds sail on. Altogether he wrote 17 marine adventure stories, two novels and dozens of short stories.

Part of his last round-the-world epic included a journey overland. He was sailing the 28-ft Henry Wagner to the South China Sea from the Indian Ocean, and the Kra Isthmus that joins Malaysia to Singapore was in the way. With a group of three disabled Thai youths, he sailed as far up the Trang River as he could. Then he enlisted an Indian elephant and the Thai army to drag the boat nine miles to the headwaters of the Ta-pee river, which flowed into the South China Sea.

People found his exploits thrilling, but some never understood what motivated him.

21

Tristan Jones said once: 'I've sailed an ocean-going craft as close to heaven as may be done until man finds water among the stars.' As an epitaph for a sailor, it will serve.

A With Nelson, he ventured into the Arctic, trying to beat the record for the farthest north any boat had got. His craft was an antique lifeboat powered by an old London Fire Brigade pumping engine.

B Like Long John Silver, he had lost a leg – though in his case the replacement was made of plastic. His sole crew was Nelson, a three-legged, one-eyed labrador he inherited when the captain of his first sailing ketch[1] died.

C 'I like being my own boss,' he used to say. 'Sailing's the only work I've ever done.'

D 'Why do you do it?' he was asked. His answer: 'You get up one day and think you would like to go to New Guinea. So you go.'

E Then he had to sail up the Amazon and, starving, hack[2] his way through the jungle swamps of the Mato Grosso. The book he wrote about those three weeks of hell in the Mato Grosso – *The Incredible Voyage* – was another Boy's Own Classic.

F Jones's most recent round-the-world voyage was from west to east – the hard way. He said the sunsets looked so much better when seen from the stern[3].

G Disabled out of the Navy when guerrillas blew up his ship in Aden, he was told he would never walk again. For most, that would have been the end of a seafaring career. For Tristan Jones, it was the start of his solo sailing.

H Though raised[4] in Wales, Jones spent most of his life sailing small boats single-handedly, and went four times round the world.

---

[1] *ketch:* small sailing boat
[2] *hack:* cut roughly
[3] *stern:* back end of a boat
[4] *raised:* brought up

Part 4

You are going to read part of a magazine article on health, with contributions from different people. Answer questions 22-35 by choosing from the people (A-E). Any of the people may be chosen more than once.

> A Tina Baines
>
> B Josephine Cartland
>
> C Francesca Lewis
>
> D Dr Andrew Page
>
> E Edward Nicholson

Which person implies or states the following opinion?

It is the government's responsibility to provide comprehensive healthcare.	22
Doctors have difficulty in meeting all the demands of their patients.	23
Individuals will need to take out insurance to cover unexpected health problems.	24
Alternative methods of medical treatment are far more successful than orthodox medicine.	25
A healthy lifestyle means that you rarely need medical help.	26 27
Healthcare provision is deteriorating.	28 29
There is more mental illness around these days, as a result of the pressures of modern life.	30
Waiting-lists for pain-relieving operations are unacceptable.	31
It is an employer's duty to provide a safe and healthy working environment.	32
It is important to look at the whole person when trying to treat a patient, not just the symptoms.	33
Scientific research has not been able to come up with solutions to all medical problems.	34 35

GOOD HEALTH TO YOU!

Most people have strong views on what makes or keeps them healthy, as well as what kind of healthcare they expect.

Tina Baines is a trained acupuncturist who has had years of experience treating all sorts of problems. She is also a qualified doctor, and this enables her to compare the two systems of oriental and western medicine. She is convinced that alternative therapies, such as acupuncture and homeopathy, bring much greater benefits to the patient than the more traditional methods prescribed by the family doctor. 'For one thing, we don't limit ourselves to examining the patient's symptoms. Our holistic approach means we consider diet, weight, previous illnesses, allergies, worries, lifestyle, everything, before we make a diagnosis.'

Josephine Cartland is 76, and has been waiting to have a hip replacement operation for six months. She is in constant pain. Recently the hospital authorities informed her that she was still near the bottom of the waiting-list. She is furious. 'Why should I have to wait like this? My husband and I have paid our taxes all our lives. I think it's up to the state to make sure we get operations, and doctors, and medicine, when we need them, whatever's wrong with us. And we shouldn't have to pay either! Do they realize what pain I'm in? I don't think they care! Things are getting worse and worse with the health service.'

Francesca Lewis is a dancer with an international ballet company. 'I must admit I hardly ever go to the doctor. I suppose it's because I really have to take care of myself in my job. We exercise a lot, and I'm very careful what I eat. I never drink or smoke, and I don't have late nights. Rather boring, but very healthy! And if I ever get ill, I don't do much about it. If it's flu, I might stay in bed for a couple of days, but if it's just a cold, I usually pay no attention – just carry on with my normal routine. I can guarantee it works!'

Dr Andrew Page is a general practitioner, with about two thousand patients in his care. He finds it a rewarding but stressful job. 'We do our best, but sometimes that doesn't seem to be enough. Patients often expect the impossible. I've lost count of the times I've been called out in the middle of the night for very trivial reasons, but even if it's just a sore throat that's ruined my night's sleep, I still have to be courteous and professional. And patients assume we can cure them, but medicine is still evolving – we haven't got all the answers yet. What people should really try to do is eat properly, take exercise and stay fit – you know the old saying, an apple a day keeps the doctor away. Then we wouldn't have such long queues in our waiting-rooms.'

Edward Nicholson is a hospital manager, whose main aim is to provide the right care for patients while keeping within a tight budget. 'Medical care has become so complicated and so expensive these days that government funding is just not sufficient any more. Hospitals cannot guarantee total healthcare for everyone. There comes a point where the state simply cannot meet the bills. In future, people will have to be prepared to cover themselves in cases of sudden or extended illness – the premiums are not unreasonable.'

He points out that current lifestyles often contribute to or cause health problems. 'We see a lot of work-related accident victims in the Casualty Department, often as a result of bosses trying to increase productivity, although there is a legal obligation on companies to protect their employees at work. Another area of concern is that of the mental ill-health suffered by a cross-section of society, because of the stress they encounter these days. The solution to these problems, whether social or medical, has not yet been found, despite the best efforts of our scientists.'

Part 1

You are going to read part of a newspaper article about coincidences. Choose from the list (A-H) the most suitable heading for each part (1-7) of the article. There is one extra heading.

> A If we want to, can we make it happen?
>
> B Hey presto! Here he is
>
> C On track for disaster
>
> D A combination of fear and panic
>
> E Is it coincidence? Or ...?
>
> F Safe information
>
> G Thought waves
>
> H What do the experts say?

IS LIFE REALLY JUST A GAME OF CHANCE?

As **Sue Carpenter** reports, there could be powerful paranormal forces at work.

> **1**

What are the chances of landing in a country of 17 million people and discovering that one of the people, with whom you had absolutely no prior connection, turns out to be a relative you never knew you had? An extraordinary coincidence? Or something more? That was exactly what happened to a friend, Clare, ten years ago. We were travelling through Australia and met up with friends of my brother's – Rob and his wife Jenny – for dinner. Small talk revealed that Jenny and Clare both had relatives who were fruit farmers in the south. Then they discovered the greatest coincidence of all. Jenny and Clare, who had never met or even heard of one another before, were second cousins.

> **2**

Coincidences have fascinated me ever since that day in Sydney. Could it be possible that there is some unknown force pulling people or events together? When we really need something and out of the blue it comes to us, have we willed it to happen? When an old friend rings up just as we're about to call them, are we sending out telepathic signals?

> **3**

Recent research has thrown up some fascinating ideas on coincidences – and the new thinking is that they are much more than just a matter of chance. Statisticians would argue that many apparently astounding incidents are more likely to occur than we would think. The probability of two people among 50 sharing a birthday is 97 per cent. And for every one-in-million chance event, such as the collision of motorcyclist Frederick Chance with driver Frederick Chance in Worcestershire in 1969, what of the 999,999 times it doesn't happen? In their *Encyclopaedia Of The Unexplained*, however, Jenny Randles and Peter Hough suggest that driving forces at the subconscious level can make a person be in a certain place at a certain time. Our inner minds guide us through a series of actions that lead us to the point where the 'coincidence' occurs.

| 4 |

There have been many apparently telepathic incidents. Chay Blyth's wife was dining at a restaurant, while her husband was thousands of miles away, braving the ocean in a catamaran. Suddenly she was overcome with nausea[1] and knew something was wrong. At that very point, she later discovered, her husband's boat had capsized[2].

| 5 |

Last year, I was on another long trip abroad, when an astonishing coincidence occurred. My travelling companion Lucy had been thinking about her ex-boyfriend, Henry Slack. As we looked around a hotel in Zanzibar, enter Henry and friend, who had, quite independently, organised a fortnight's holiday there. It was almost as if Lucy had conjured him up by the power of her thoughts.

| 6 |

People frequently report a sudden urge to contact someone close to them just before they die – although they have no conscious knowledge of the impending death. As a trainee officer at Sandhurst, John Dawes woke up one night and told his wife that, in his dream, his mother had been trying to give him the combination of her safe. Next morning, his brother rang from Kent to tell him their mother had died. Just before passing away, she had tried to mouth the combination numbers of her safe.

| 7 |

Jenny Randles maintains that even non-personal twists of fate are linked on a level where space and time do not exist. Consider this case, for instance. In 1981, British Rail had a call from a woman who had a vision of a fatal crash, involving engine number 47216. Two years later, an identical accident happened – to train 47299. A trainspotter noticed, however, that this was not the train's original number. So impressed had BR been by the call, that it had tried to avert disaster by changing the train's number – from 47216 to 47299.

[1] *nausea:* a feeling of sickness
[2] *capsized:* overturned in the water

Part 2

You are going to read part of a magazine article about a reporter, Sue Lloyd-Roberts.
For questions 8-15, choose the correct answer (A, B, C, or D).

My work as a BBC TV foreign correspondent means that I spend about one week in five abroad. I specialise in human rights and environmental stories and travel alone, as a one-woman crew. But when I'm not abroad, I'm at home in north London, with my two children, researching and preparing for my next trip.

5 I'm often asked why I do such a crazy job when I've got children, but in actual fact I'm outside the school gates far more often than a high-powered woman who's, say, an MP or a company executive because I can dictate my own schedules. I don't do sudden news stories and choose never to go into war zones, so the danger is minimal.

Working alone as both reporter and cameraman suits me perfectly because I do very little eating
10 and sleeping on trips and I don't think a crew would appreciate having to fit in with me. I also cut down the amount of time I'm away from home by using the nights to travel. In Iraq recently I slept through two nine-hour car journeys across the desert, so I could hit the ground running when I arrived.

At home, my day begins with BBC1's Breakfast News at 7 a.m. If I'm in it, the children sit on
15 the end of my bed and watch with me, although they're usually more concerned about where their breakfast is. When they've gone to school, I do 30 lengths of the local pool – my only keep-fit activity – before starting work. I'm always planning several future trips and have lunch with various opposition leaders, former diplomats and their fellow workers three or four times a week. London is a very good place to establish these contacts.

20 The day before I travel is always an at-home day, for packing, checking my equipment and spending time with the children. I have to clean my camera – a top-of-the-range Sony UXI – and make sure I've got all the necessary videotapes, lenses, bulbs and batteries. I travel so lightly that I could easily be mistaken for a tourist, although if I'm in a country where they're likely to be a bit suspicious, I leave my tripod behind. I'm sure that it helps to be a woman because whenever I'm
25 questioned by the authorities, I play the middle-aged housewife and they usually let me go.

I'm not a domesticated animal so our nanny, Julie, usually cooks the evening meal. But on a pre-travel day I give her the evening off so we can be alone as a family. I'm sure it's sometimes difficult for the kids, but there is a plus side as they're quite involved in what I do and have met all sorts of interesting people at our house. My daughter has the best foreign doll collection in
30 London! But I'm prepared for the possibility that one day they'll turn round and say, "Where were you, Mum?"

8 Which of the following statements is true?

  A Sue spends most of her time working abroad.
  B She only travels with one cameraman.
  C When at home in London, she devotes all her time to her children.
  D She concentrates on particular issues in her reports.

9 What does she think about her career and motherhood?

  A It's madness trying to be a mother *and* a foreign correspondent.
  B Her timetable is flexible so she can be available for her children.
  C Having children gives her insight into situations of conflict.
  D She would really prefer to be a high-powered careerwoman.

10 How has she adapted physically to her job?

   A She needs very little food or sleep.
   B She sleeps while travelling in order to save money.
   C She needs exercise when she arrives in a new place.
   D She is psychologically unsuited to working in a team.

11 How does she spend her day at home?

   A She gets involved in various sporting activities.
   B She often has lunch with members of the government.
   C She spends a lot of time getting information for future projects.
   D The first thing is to get breakfast ready for the children.

12 Does being a woman help her in her job?

   A No, she has to check and clean all her equipment herself.
   B Yes, because the authorities abroad are not likely to take her seriously.
   C Yes, because she just looks like a tourist.
   D No, she can't carry her tripod and sometimes leaves it behind.

13 What arrangements for childcare has she made?

   A Her parents regularly collect the children from school.
   B She pays a babysitter, Julie, to cook supper every day.
   C She takes sole responsibility for childcare all the time she is at home.
   D She has a nanny who comes whenever necessary.

14 What are the effects of her job on her children?

   A They are gaining an awareness of the issues she specialises in.
   B They often complain about her absences.
   C They both have an excellent collection of souvenirs.
   D They can sometimes be difficult to cope with.

15 How do you think she feels about her job?

   A worried she might lose it
   B hopeful that she can change it later
   C enthusiastic and committed
   D fed up with the problems involved

Part 3

You are going to read part of an article on current working conditions. Seven sentences have been removed from the text. Choose from sentences A-H the one which fits each gap (16-22). There is one extra sentence which you do not need to use.

WORK TILL YOU DROP

16 I can see a jumbled montage of postcards on a pin-board, a gaunt plant with crinkled leaves and a faint glimmer of daylight between drawn blinds. **17** All around there is an anarchic mess of documents, as if I have stumbled into a refugee camp for paperwork: books piled high, notebooks filled and flung to one side, magazines half read and covered in a fine layer of dust. The room flickers in the glow of a fluorescent light.

Air-conditioning hums in the background. Telephones screech. A colleague is shouting down the phone. **18** A third chatters to herself as she writes, like an excited song-thrush[1].

It is just another day in *The Guardian*'s Farringdon Road offices, and I'm feeling fine. My nose is doing the police interrogator's double act: one nostril blocked, the other pouring. My back aches, leg muscles are atrophying[2] from disuse and my brain feels like it has been cling-wrapped in sandpaper.

19 After you have scrambled into the office today and slumped breathless into a chair, sit back. Look around. Savour the air. Listen to the cacophony[3]. If you still feel happy, you are lucky. The physical world of work, it seems, is eroding the strength of many of us.

Today the Health and Safety Executive brings out a report that aims to spread the message that offices can seriously damage your health. **20** The HSE says that an edifice can be diagnosed sick where staff complain of being ill more commonly than might be reasonably expected. **21** Seven out of ten office workers reported symptoms at work such as runny noses, tight chests and lethargy[4] – symptoms that vanished the instant they quit the building. **22** Elements at work such as dodgy[5] air-conditioning, low humidity, excessive heat and dust, can act as a sort of poison, making employees tired and worn out, irritating their eyes, noses and throats, and constricting breath.

[1] *song-thrush:* bird with attractive song
[2] *atrophying:* losing strength, wasting away
[3] *cacophony:* noise

[4] *lethargy:* lack of energy
[5] *dodgy:* defective

A Company auditors complain that overheads are rising, due to increased energy costs.

B Another thumps his keyboard as a child bashes a piano.

C In an attempt to explain these grumblings, academics have come up with the notion that illness can also be reflected externally in the fabric and structure of a building.

D Just how frequent such complaints have become is highlighted in a joint study by architecture schools in Cardiff and London.

E If you think that sounds bad, pause and reflect on your own working conditions.

F I am sitting in a room with a view.

G Following terminology coined in the United States, it calls the malaise Sick Building Syndrome.

H Banks of desks, screens, faxes and photocopiers stretch into the distance.

Part 4

You are going to read some extracts from an article on London. Choose the correct answers (A-I) to questions 23-33. Any of the answers may be chosen more than once. For questions 34 and 35, select the best answer from A, B, C or D.

Which extract tells you

about the dress code in a certain store? | 23 |

the size of two of the capital's parks? | 24 |

where to find a genuine old pub? | 25 |

which nightclubs are fashionable at the moment? | 26 |

the best time to go to a pantomime? | 27 |

about sightseeing boat trips? | 28 |

where the illuminations can be seen? | 29 |

Where can you find

advice on accommodation? | 30 |

advice on buying theatre tickets? | 31 |

information about the New Year sales? | 32 | 33 |

34 What do you think the writer of the article is personally most interested in?

A eating fast food
B walking in the countryside
C visiting old museums
D staying in hotels

35 What information is **not** included in these extracts?

A where to book tickets for a musical
B rules in force at the Burlington Arcade
C information on the bus network
D a recommendation of somewhere to eat

LONDON IN WINTER

ROBIN MEAD discovers that the capital has much to offer at this time of the year.

A

There's nothing nicer on a fine winter's afternoon than to put on a stout pair of shoes and take a brisk country walk.

London's favourite 'country' walk takes you across the former royal hunting grounds of Kensington Gardens, Hyde Park, Green Park and St James's Park, more or less in a straight line from Queensway tube station almost down to the banks of the River Thames in Westminster. The vast open spaces dotted with gleaming lakes sprawl across central London like a great green carpet and you only cross a couple of main roads during the entire walk.

The sheer size of this city-centre playground doesn't really register until you walk across it. There are entire countries smaller than this! And no, that's not an exaggeration: Kensington Gardens and Hyde Park together cover some 600 acres – an area larger than the principality of Monaco.

The nation's capital doesn't close down just because it is winter, any more than it closes down after dark. After all, it has got a reputation to live up to: that of being one of the most exciting cities in the world.

B

In December, the Christmas lights turn Oxford Street and Regent Street into a glittering fairyland; carol singers gather around the giant tree erected in Trafalgar Square; and the big stores compete with one another to see which of them can produce the most magical window display.

"The biggest shopping centre in the world is right here, in the heart of London," declares John Poppleton, chairman of the London Chamber of Commerce. He is referring to the area bounded by Oxford Street, Regent Street, Bond Street and Piccadilly – and he has a point. Whatever you want to buy, you can find it in that huge, golden rectangle. And, come the January sales, you can buy it cheaply too.

The sales have become an institution – and a massive tourist attraction. Harrods alone sees its average daily total of 35,000 customers boosted to a breathtaking 300,000 on the first day of its January sale.

C

The big stores have become so important a part of the London shopping scene that they can even afford to make their own rules. Harrods won't let you into the store if you are wearing cut-off shorts or a T-shirt, or if you are carrying a rucksack. And, if you think that's strict, try the Regency-style Burlington Arcade, off Piccadilly, where a security force of three beadles is on hand to ensure that there is "no running, no whistling, no singing and no merrymaking."

D

If you are visiting London and want to know what to buy and where, or – just as importantly at this time of year – details about the January sales, then the London Tourist Board has a new London Shopping Newsline (tel 0891 505478), with all the information you should need for the price of a normal telephone call.

E

London's other 'traditional' attraction, besides shopping, is theatre-going. This is at its best over Christmas and the New Year when the pantomime season is in full swing. The range of shows covers everything from top musicals to Shakespearean dramas. The latter are more interesting now that the Elizabethan-style Globe Theatre has opened at Bankside.

For tickets to West End shows, try the half-price booth in Leicester Square: it opens at noon to sell tickets for that evening's performances. Alternatively, the Tourist Information Centres at Victoria, Liverpool Street Station and Heathrow all sell theatre tickets, although they charge full price. Add the jazz at Ronnie Scott's in Soho and a few nightspots (Limelight, Legends and the Wag are the 'in' places), and that's your after-dark entertainment looked after.

F

The Thames can look beautiful in winter and there are countless attractions lining its banks to provide more than ample diversion. Or you can catch a riverboat from Charing Cross Pier, either upstream to Hampton Court or downstream to Greenwich. This ancient borough has given itself a trendy new nickname these days – Greenwich Village. At least our Greenwich is a villagey sort of place.

G

Museums include Sir John Soane's unique and extraordinary collection of art and antiquities at No 13 Lincoln's Inn Fields (tel 0171 405 2107), Florence Nightingale's Museum at St Thomas' Hospital (tel 0171 620 0374), and the Bank of England Museum (tel 0171 601 5545). But don't miss old favourites such as the Natural History Museum (tel 0171 938 9123), the Science Museum (tel 0171 938 8000) and the Victoria and Albert Museum (tel 0171 938 8500).

H

If you are not a regular visitor to London, the choice of things to do can be bewildering. So can the selection of restaurants and the number of places to stay. The important rule is, don't be guided by price. When it comes to eating and sleeping, price is not always an indication of quality.

I

After a hard day's sightseeing and before you head back to your luxury digs, down a glass of ale or two in the spit-and-sawdust atmosphere of Ye Olde Cheshire Cheese in Fleet Street or a steak-and-red-wine dinner at Rowley's, in Jermyn Street. You can find plastic pubs and hamburger joints anywhere, but these are the real thing.

What's more, they won't charge you tourist prices. Which is good, because tomorrow is another shopping day. "And in London," a tourist board spokeswoman told me, "going shopping is just as good as going sightseeing."

Part 1

You are going to read a newspaper article about a recent invention. Choose from the list (A-H) the sentence which best summarises each part (1-7) of the article. There is one extra sentence.

A The inventor hopes to make a fortune from it.

B There has been a recent development in the fight against car crime.

C Equipment installed in the vehicle will help police to identify and stop the car.

D The great advantage of this new device is that thieves will be caught unawares.

E The initial price of the immobilising equipment will be reasonable.

F Stolen cars will be traced and tracked by the owner.

G Information about stolen cars can be registered through a new hi-tech procedure.

H Mr Webster was keen to help police catch more car thieves.

THIEVES CUT OFF IN THEIR CRIME

by Ray Massey – Motoring Correspondent

1

An inventor working in his garden shed has developed a device which enables police to track and then stop stolen cars by remote control. A satellite signal to an electronic gadget hidden in the vehicle locks the doors as it is automatically slowed down, leaving the baffled thief helpless inside. The prototype for the cigarette pack-sized immobilising device was tested on an old Volvo. Now its inventors and the police hope the Home Office will approve it for use on public roads to enable a manufacturer to go into full production.

2

The system, called KeepSafe, will enable a car owner who discovers his vehicle has been stolen to retrieve it – and probably trap the thief – with one phone call. He or she will be answered by a recorded voice asking them to key in a special code number, using the phone's keypad. This gives access to the system. They will then connect to the Police National Computer by pressing a set of numbers which automatically register the car as stolen.

3

An officer, seeing the message flash up on his screen, will start the next stage of the process. The gadget in the car will be activated by a signal from police. This will initially enable the car to be traced and tracked by satellite. Once police are satisfied there is no danger to other road-users, a coded call to the engine immobiliser will slow down the car in stages of 10 or 20 mph until it comes to a halt – with doors and windows locked.

4

Police patrol officers, alerted over the stolen car's progress so they can establish a safe place for it to be stopped, will be waiting to arrest the thief. Inventor Niall Webster, 39, said: 'As a member of the public I was fed up with all these people attempting to steal cars. I thought, surely we can do something to increase the recovery rates. The beauty of being a smaller-scale inventor is that I can lock myself in the garden shed to come up with ideas. This is the classic garden shed invention.'

> **5**

Security consultant Colin Goodwin, who helped Mr Webster develop the system, said: 'As security devices become ever more sophisticated, car thieves are becoming increasingly resourceful. Existing alarms and immobilisers mean the thieves cannot start the car. So instead, they are resorting to hijackings or breaking into homes to steal the keys. The joy of our system is that, even if they succeed in getting the keys, they can still be stopped. The thief or joyrider doesn't know the police are chasing, and will be at a loss when the power starts to gradually fade from the engine.'

> **6**

The inventors believe that, at a cost of around £300, it will prove popular with all car owners.

> **7**

Mr Webster has set up a firm in Grimsby to develop the device. He hopes the gadget will turn him and his partners into millionaires, and is negotiating with a number of manufacturers.

Part 2

You are going to read an extract from *As I Walked Out One Midsummer Morning* by Laurie Lee. For questions 8-14, choose the correct answer (A, B, C or D).

The stooping figure of my mother, waist-deep in the grass and caught there like a piece of sheep's wool, was the last I saw of my country home as I left it to discover the world. She stood old and bent at the top of the bank, silently watching me go, one gnarled red hand raised in farewell and blessing, not questioning why I went. At the bend of the road I looked back again and saw the gold
5 light die behind her; then I turned the corner, passed the village school, and closed that part of my life for ever.

It was a bright Sunday morning in early June, the right time to be leaving home. My three sisters and a brother had already gone before me; two other brothers had yet to make up their minds. They were still sleeping that morning, but my mother had got up early and cooked me a heavy
10 breakfast, had stood wordlessly while I ate it, her hand on my chair, and had then helped me pack up my few belongings. There had been no fuss, no appeals, no attempts at advice or persuasion, only a long and searching look. Then, with my bags on my back, I'd gone out into the early sunshine and climbed through the long wet grass to the road.

It was 1934. I was nineteen years old, still soft at the edges, but with a confident belief in good
15 fortune. I carried a small rolled-up tent, a violin in a blanket, a change of clothes, a tin of treacle biscuits and some cheese. I was excited, knowing I had far to go; but not, as yet, how far. As I left home that morning and walked away from the sleeping village, it never occurred to me that others had done this before me.

I was propelled, of course, by the traditional forces that had sent many generations along this
20 road – by the small tight valley closing in around me, stifling the breath with its mossy mouth, the cottage walls narrowing, the local girls whispering, 'Marry, and settle down.'

And now I was on my journey, in a pair of thick boots and with a stick in my hand. Naturally, I was going to London, which lay a hundred miles to the east; and it seemed equally obvious that I should go on foot. But first, as I'd never yet seen the sea, I thought I'd walk to the coast and
25 find it. This would add another hundred miles to my journey, going by way of Southampton. But I had all the summer and all time to spend.

As I tramped through the dust towards the Wiltshire Downs a growing reluctance weighed me down. Through the solitary morning and afternoon I found myself longing for some opposition or rescue, for the sound of hurrying footsteps coming after me and family voices calling me back.

30 None came. I was free. The day's silence said, Go where you will. It's all yours. You asked for it. It's up to you now. You're on your own and nobody's going to stop you.

8 How would you describe the writer's mother?

A tolerant and understanding
B careworn and complaining
C lively and sociable, but no longer young
D argumentative and elderly

9 The writer says that his mother

A tried to persuade him to stay.
B encouraged him to leave.
C asked him why he was leaving.
D accepted his decision to leave.

10 As he started on his journey, he

A felt sure he would be able to manage on his own.
B thought he was just like all the others who had left home.
C felt sad at leaving.
D knew exactly where he was going.

11 His reason for leaving home was that

A his girlfriend had asked him to marry her.
B he wanted to find a bigger house to live in.
C it was a family tradition to move out at nineteen.
D he wanted to broaden his experience.

12 He decided to go first

A a hundred miles east, to London.
B to the coast, to see the sea.
C to London and then Southampton.
D on foot and then by sea.

13 When nobody hurried after him to call him back, he

A had an exciting sense of freedom.
B experienced a feeling of regret.
C was unwilling to return.
D felt even more enthusiastic about his journey.

14 What does 'it' in 'you asked for it' (line 30) refer to?

A the countryside
B the silence
C freedom
D his family

Part 3

You are going to read part of an article about Venice. Six paragraphs have been removed. Choose from paragraphs A-G the one which fits each gap (15-20). There is one extra paragraph which you do not need to use.

VENICE

To begin with, Venice is small. The sweep of the vistas across the Venetian Lagoon, the immense, moody arc of the sky, the grandiose facades all give the illusion of amplitude[1]; it comes as a shock to learn that Venice, dense as a diamond, covers a mere three square miles.

| 15 |

Walking, as much as the surrounding water, dictates the shape of Venetian life; the reasonable pace, the sudden street-corner encounters with friends, the pause to talk.

| 16 |

They like to say their city is like a living room.

| 17 |

In a word, yes, though the rate has slowed, mainly because the pumping of groundwater for industries on the mainland has been stopped. The catastrophic flood of November 4, 1966 inundated parts of the city with as much as four feet of water for 24 hours.

[1] *amplitude:* large size

| 18 |

But today a rising tide of troubles is more likely to swamp the city. A new sense of desperation seems to have taken hold. Businesses have moved out; the population has shrunk over the past 30 years from 138,000 to a mere 70,000.

| 19 |

Most Venetians have known one another from birth. They are also essentially island people, living offshore in their own self-contained universe.

| 20 |

"Every time I leave Venice, I have not only psychological pain but physical pain too. Deep pain. It's stupid; I can't explain it. When you're away, you feel that something is lost. Because here people are different, relationships are different, houses are different, *everything* is different. When I see the lagoon from the plane, I thank God that I'm back."

A Since then, a tremendous international effort has been made to repair the palaces and churches, restore the works of art and protect the surrounding lagoon from future tidal calamity.

B Among the many things the Venetians love about their town – no cars, virtually no crime – this intimacy is the best.

C "I don't like going to the mainland," one elderly gondolier told me. "And I only ever go by boat."

D 1,500 people a year leave Venice, especially young families unwilling to cope with the cost of living, finding a good job and an affordable house or apartment. These are the unglamorous facts of life in any city.

E You could walk from one end to the other in an hour. And you will walk, because the streets are usually the size of an average sidewalk[2].

F "Venice is a place that overwhelms you," Clarenza Catullo said frankly as we sat at dinner one winter evening. She is a senior assistant at a museum; her Venetian parents moved to the mainland, but she moved back.

G Is Venice still sinking? This is the question everybody outside Venice seems to ask.

[2] *sidewalk:* pavement

Part 4

You are going to read some short texts giving you information on New Zealand. Choose the correct answers (A-I) to questions 21-33. Any of the answers may be chosen more than once. For questions 34 and 35, select the best answer from A, B, C, or D.

Where can you

participate in a crime investigation weekend?   **21** ☐

see an authentic tribal canoe?   **22** ☐

be caught unawares by a sudden storm?   **23** ☐

visit a museum without paying anything?   **24** ☐

find a large reduction in entrance fees for children?   **25** ☐

see some of the ancient trees native to New Zealand?   **26** ☐

Which place

is easy to find?   **27** ☐

is full of unusual geological features?   **28** ☐

is officially protected from industrial use?   **29** ☐

might be recommended by a doctor?   **30** ☐

offers the widest variety of sporting activities?   **31** ☐

offers the most relaxing means of transport?   **32** ☐

was visited by two different explorers?   **33** ☐

34 Where do you think these mini-texts come from?

   A   a magazine on current affairs
   B   a geography textbook
   C   a newspaper article on natural history
   D   a guidebook

35 Which is **not** true about this information?

   A   It helps you decide which places to visit.
   B   It tells you about the history of New Zealand.
   C   It suggests new sporting activities to try.
   D   It gives you details of accommodation available in each place.

A

Auckland

If you're only going to see one thing in Auckland, see one of Auckland's magnificent museums. The Auckland Museum in the Domain has a tremendous display of Maori artefacts and culture: pride of place goes to a magnificent 25-metre-long war canoe, but there are many other examples of the Maoris' arts and lifestyle. The museum also houses a fine display of South Pacific items and NZ wildlife, and displays thousands of other interesting objects from around the world.

It is open from 10 am to 5 pm daily; admission is free.

B

Waipoua Kauri Forest

The road north enters the Waipoua Kauri Forest 50 km out of Dargaville. The Waipoua Kauri Forest Sanctuary, proclaimed in 1952 after much public pressure, is the largest remnant of the once extensive kauri forests of northern New Zealand. There is no cutting of mature kauri trees nowadays, except under extraordinary circumstances such as for the carving of a Maori canoe.

The road through the forest passes by some splendid huge kauris. Turn off to the forest lookout just after you enter the park – it was once a fire lookout and offers a spectacular view.

C

Otorohanga

The well-signposted Otorohanga Kiwi House is the town's main attraction and worth a visit. In a kiwi house night and day are reversed, so you can watch the kiwis in daytime under artificial moonlight. There are also various other native birds. The walk-in aviary is the largest in New Zealand.

The Kiwi House is open from 10 am to 5 pm every day, except from June to August when it closes at 4 pm. The last admission is half an hour before closing time. Admission $6 (children $2).

D

Waitomo

Waitomo (population 300) is famous for its limestone caves; the whole region is riddled with caves and strange limestone formations. Tours through the Waitomo Cave (also called the Glow-worm Cave), the Ruakuri Cave and the Aranui Cave have been feature attractions for decades. In recent years a whole new batch of activities has cropped up – organised caving expeditions, rafting through caves, abseiling and various combinations of the three, plus horse trekking, white water rafting and more.

E

Mount Egmont/Taranaki

Due to its easy accessibility, Mt Taranaki ranks as the 'most climbed' mountain in New Zealand. Nevertheless, hiking on this mountain holds definite dangers and should not be undertaken lightly. The principal hazard is the erratic weather, which can change from warm, sunny shorts weather to raging gales and white-out conditions amazingly quickly and unexpectedly; snow can come at any time of year on the mountain, even in summer. In good conditions hiking around the mountain, or even to the summit, can be reasonably easy, but the mountain has claimed over 50 lives. Don't be put off, but don't be deceived.

F

Thames

Twice a month the Brian Boru Hotel becomes the scene of a murder, and each of the 30 to 45 guests is a suspect, when the Agatha Christie weekend takes place. Guests arrive on Friday evening for dinner and spend the Saturday on guided visits. On Saturday evening they don fancy-dress costumes and the mystery begins. The race is on to guess 'whodunnit'. The successful detective wins $200. On Sunday everyone joins in a 'post-mortem' over a big breakfast.

The price of $300 covers everything for the whole weekend, including the use of a fancy-dress costume if you don't happen to have your own.

G

Whitianga

The pleasant Whitianga area of Mercury Bay has a long history, by NZ standards. The Polynesian explorer Kupe landed near here around 950 AD.

Mercury Bay was given its modern name by Captain Cook when he observed the transit of Mercury while anchored in the bay in November 1769.

The town is a big game-fishing base for tuna, marlin, mako (blue pointer shark), thresher shark and kingfish.

H

Lake Taupo

Three boats specialise in cruises on the lake: the *Barbary,* the *Spirit of Musick* and the *Ernest Kemp.*

All three boats offer similar cruises, visiting a modern Maori rock carving beside the lake. The carving is on private land so it cannot be reached on foot; the only way to see it is by boat. In summer all three boats offer morning, afternoon and evening cruises; they sail in winter too but usually only once or twice a day. The cruises last about 2½ to 3 hours; the cost is $20 (children $10) on all the boats.

I

Waikite

Waikite Thermal Mineral Baths is an open-air natural mineral pool (39°C) with medicinal mineral waters, out in Waikite, a rural area. To get there, go 30 km south on SH 5 (the highway to Taupo), to a signposted turn-off which is opposite the turn-off to Waiotapu. The pool is another six km down this road. It is open every day from 10 am to 9.30 pm; admission is $4 (children $2).

Mount Taranaki

SECTION 1

Unit 1

A The writer is describing his/her daily journey to school.

B It is important to choose the right kind of holiday.

C An old woman is comparing her past with the present.

D Traditional ways of farming in Spain are being lost because of (the impact of) tourism.

E There have been cuts in water supplies because of recent drought/very dry conditions in Europe, so people and water companies are now more interested in saving water.

F The authorities in Paris are introducing a number of measures in order to reduce air pollution.

Unit 2

A 1C   2A   3B   4B/D   5E   6B/C   7C   8G   9F   10B

B 1 Camp Beaumont
    2 Canadian Affair
    3 Chinese State Circus, Preston Park, Brighton
    4 Annual Festival of Scottish Dance, Wyeside Arts Centre, Builth Wells
    5 Rough Magic
    6 Festival of English Food & Wine, Leeds Castle, Maidstone
    7 Hoseasons
    8 David Austin
    9 Farmer, 40
   10 Adams Antiques Fair, Royal Horticultural Society Halls, London

Progress Test 1

1 Britain/England
2 1795: Prince George and Princess Caroline got married; 1820, King George III died and his son was crowned King.
3 George III, father of George IV; George IV was married to Princess Caroline of Brunswick; they had a daughter, Princess Charlotte.
4 It was thought to be madness, but was probably a blood disorder which could have been cured with today's drugs.
5 Westminster Abbey.
6 To get a large amount of money from Parliament.

Feedback

1 Skimming is reading quickly for the gist or general meaning, while scanning means looking quickly for the answers to particular questions.

2 a to become king
     b to use
     c periods/attacks
     d passed on in the blood from your parents/grandparents
     e illness/disease
     f at that time
     g madness
     h ruler in the King's place
     i crowning ceremony
     j regular payment of money
     k a child who will inherit
     l take a softer attitude
     m not large or expensive
     n bad/wicked
     o exciting

Examples of past perfect: *he had been waiting* a long time (line 1), His father ... *had suffered* from repeated bouts ... (line 2), his son had *been declared* Prince Regent (line 6), He *had married* her in 1795 (line 10), she *had been* guilty ... (line 19).

Unit 3

A 1 A much/a good deal
B connected
C go up and down
D punctuality/ability to be trusted

2 A it is hard to tell the difference between them
B lower priced products/buying cheaper tickets
C people who prefer to pay more to be sure they will travel on time without problems
D with limited money

3 You don't have to be at the airport as early; the plane is more likely to take off on time. The correct answer is A.

4 D The distractors are B and C.

B 1 A area of homes built by very poor people on the edge of a city, using any materials they can find
B rubbish
C done willingly, from choice
D to get on

2 A have proved
B a determination to do everything in a way that protects the environment
C a continuous moving line
D part of the road used only by buses

3 D

4 C

5 B

Unit 4

A *(These are only suggested answers – others may be appropriate.)*
1 Girlfriend and boyfriend?
2 Their relationship? Breaking up? His personality problems?
3 Probably Liz, as she is taking the initiative.
4 a) tense, vulnerable, a worrier   b) self-centred, cool   c) American?
5 Probably they always go to a certain seminar on Tuesdays.
6 See you later.
7-9 need subjective answers.

B 1 Yes: 'At first glance the village looked just the same.'
2 In the past: 'It seemed a waste, somehow.'
3 Moira has been locked up by someone, or at least appears rather isolated in her room. The Baron's ghost has appeared several times and attacked or killed two people already.
4 She is cold and also dreading the possible appearance of the Baron's ghost.
5 To Edinburgh, to visit her mother or other elderly female relative.
6 Both working, busy lifestyles, possibly too busy to talk.
7 a) worried, hard-working, caring   b) exhausted, hard-working   c) enthusiastic, careful

Progress Test 2

1B   2C   3A   4C

Feedback

2   a   bullfighter
    b   accepted
    c   stopped
    d   college
    e   finished her college education
    f   accepts unwillingly
    g   hard, severe
    h   bullfighting
    i   very masculine, male dominated
    j   fight
    k   only
    l   have children

Unit 5

B   *Suggested answers:* chocoholic, felt at home, ancient Mayan civilisation, Central America, sophisticated culture, chocolate, central role, a drink, a form of currency, cacao bean, three thousand years, a drink, most of that time.

C   1   Australia
    2   mouth-watering, delicious
    3   Lizard Island
    4   Lady Elliott Island
    5   Dunk Island
    6   Lizard Island
    7   Fraser Island

D   1   north-west India
    2   before 1500
    3   Egyptian
    4   Romany
    5   education and healthcare
    6   90,000

Unit 6

A   1C   2A

B   1B   2A

C   1C   2B

D   1D   2C   3B   4F   5A

Progress Test 3

1D   2B   3A   4H   5F   6C   7E

Feedback

1   a   substance found in animal fats which can contribute to heart disease
    b   all over
    c   ordered as part of medical advice or treatment
    d   in danger
    e   something produced during the making of the main product
    f   wood/timber

g   being very enthusiastic about
h   another delivery of goods
i   thrown away
j   able to be dissolved
k   eaten/drunk
l   easily changed into a different form

Unit 7

A 1C   2E   3D   4A   5B   6F   7H

B 1I   2A   3C   4B   5D   6H   7G   8J   9E   10F

C A 1F   2F   3I   4F   5I   6I   7F

   B 1F   2F   3F   4F   5I   6F   7I   8I   9F   10I

D 1 Notice, warning/advice about fire, formal
   2 Note to flatmate, giving phone message and other information, informal
   3 Advertisement, watches, formal
   4 Instruction booklet, TV, formal
   5 Note to workmates, theft of sandwiches, informal

Unit 8

A 1G   2E   3C   4A   5D   6F

B 1C   2E   3A   4B   5A/D/E/F   6A/D/E/F   7A/D/E/F   8A/D/E/F

Progress Test 4

1F   2A   3H   4G   5C   6D   7E

Feedback

1 d

2 To decide which to buy, ordering by post.

3 a using electricity, not batteries
   b take off the skin
   c light enough to carry
   d strong
   e put on
   f feeding
   g joins/stitching
   h looks like mahogany wood
   i dearly loved
   j in pieces for you to put together
   k what is needed for the recipe
   l with no effort or difficulty

SECTION 2

Unit 9

A 1D 2F 3B 4C 5A

B 1E 2F 3H 4D 5G 6B 7A

Progress Test 5

1H 2F 3I 4A 5B 6G 7D 8C

Unit 10

A 1D 2A 3C 4A 5D 6B

B 1D 2A 3B 4B 5C 6C

Progress Test 6

1A 2D 3B 4C 5D 6C 7A

Unit 11

A 1E 2G 3B 4C 5F 6A

B 1C 2H 3E 4F 5D 6G 7A

Progress Test 7

1B 2D 3H 4A 5G 6E 7F

Unit 12

A 1B/F 2B/F 3D/E 4D/E 5F/H 6F/H 7D/F 8D/F 9A
  10E 11D 12C/G 13C/G 14B 15C

B 1B/C 2B/C 3A/H 4A/H 5D/F 6D/F 7A/E/G 8A/E/G
  9A/E/G 10H 11A/G 12A/G 13F 14G 15E 16D 17A

Progress Test 8

1G 2C 3H 4B/D 5B/D 6A/G 7A/G 8B 9B/F/G
10B/F/G 11B/F/G 12C/E 13C/E 14D 15C

SECTION 3

Unit 13

A 1D 2H 3C 4B 5G 6A 7F

B 1C 2A 3D 4B 5G 6E 7F

Unit 14

A 1C 2A 3D 4C 5A 6C 7A 8D

B 1B 2C 3D 4A 5C 6C 7D

Unit 15

A 1D 2H 3F 4C 5G 6E 7B

B 1C 2E 3G 4D 5A 6F 7B

Unit 16

A 1A 2B 3D 4E 5C 6A 7A 8E 9C 10B 11A 12D 13B 14C

B 1D 2F 3C 4E 5E 6A 7B 8A/D/E 9A/D/E 10A/D/E

11A/B/E/F 12A/B/E/F 13A/B/E/F 14A/B/E/F 15D/E 16D/E

17A/E/F 18A/E/F 19A/E/F 20D

SECTION 4

Practice Test 1

Part 1
1G 2F 3B 4E 5A 6H 7C

Part 2
8A 9B 10C 11C 12D 13D 14A 15C

Part 3
16G 17H 18E 19D 20C 21A 22B

Part 4
23C 24B 25E 26A 27D 28C 29B 30D 31A 32E 33C 34B 35E

Practice Test 2

Part 1
1D 2A 3E 4G 5H 6F 7C

Part 2
8D 9B 10C 11D 12A 13D 14B

Part 3
15B 16A 17H 18G 19F 20E 21D

Part 4
22B 23D 24E 25A 26C 27D 28B 29E 30E 31B 32E 33A 34D 35E

Practice Test 3

Part 1
1E 2A 3H 4G 5B 6F 7C

Part 2
8D 9B 10A 11C 12B 13D 14A 15C

Part 3
16F 17H 18B 19E 20G 21D 22C

Part 4
23C 24A 25I 26E 27E 28F 29B 30H 31E 32B/D

33B/D 34B 35C

Practice Test 4

Part 1
1B 2G 3C 4H 5D 6E 7A

Part 2
8A 9D 10A 11D 12B 13B 14C

Part 3
15E 16B 17G 18A 19D 20F

Part 4
21F 22A 23E 24A 25C 26B 27C 28D 29B 30I 31D 32H 33G 34D 35D